Finding My Own Nuruk

Written by **Kim Hyuck Rae**

Finding My Own Nuruk

발 행 | 2023년 12월 22일
저 자 | 김혁래
편집자 | 박지은
펴낸이 | 한건희
펴낸곳 | 주식회사 부크크
출판사등록 | 2014.07.15(제2014-16호)
주 소 | 서울특별시 금천구 가산디지털1로 119 SK트윈타워 A동 305호
전 화 | 1670-8316
이메일 | info@bookk.co.kr
ISBN | 979-11-410-5974-3
www.bookk.co.kr

K-Sool does not become more delicious just because it has been brewed for a long time. Even first-time K-Sool brewers can brew delicious K-Sool if they have a good recipe. But when K-Sool goes wrong, if you don't know the cause, you experience more failures and most people give up on having their own K-Sool.

This book will serve as a guide for anyone new to K-Sool. It will give you hope that you can have your own Nuruk, your own K-Sool.
Let's leave home like martial arts novel, become masters of K-Sool, and enjoy the journey back home.

2023. 05. 30

Director of Korea Gayangju Research Institute Ryu In-soo

어떻게 영문으로 번역해야 할까?

'나만의 누룩 찾기'라는 내 이야기를 들려주리라 마음 먹었을 때부터 그 대상이 세계인이었으면 좋겠단 생각을 했다. 술은 만국 공통 언어고 모두를 친구로 만드는 마법을 지녔다. K-Pop, K-Drama, K-Food에 열광하는 모든 이들이 한국 술(K-Sool)을 반길 거라는 확신도 있었다.

하지만 이런 바램은 내 책 첫 장을 번역하며 좌절로 바뀌었다. 도무지 한국 술과 관련된 용어를 어떻게 번역해야 할 지 모르겠는 거다. 예를 들어 한국 술은, 미생물을 여러 번 키워 맛과 향을 깊게 할 수 있는데, 이 때 처음 빚는 술을 '밑술'이라 한다. 밑술의 '밑'은 '물체의 아래나 아래쪽'을 의미하니 '밑술'이라면 영어로 Bottom Liquor 또는 Basement Liquor 정도로 해석할 수 있지만 모든 용어를 이런 식으로 변경하거나 매번 의미를 설명할 수 없는 노릇.(밑술에 추가하는 술을 '덧술'이라 하는데, '덧'은 '거듭' 또는 '겹친'다는 의미니 영어로 Addition Liquor나 Overlap Liquor라 할 수 지만, 갈수록 태산이다.)

그런 측면에서 이웃 나라 일본의 양조 용어 쓰임새가 좋은 참고가 되었다. 일본 술 사케의 경우 밑술을 슈보(酒母) 또는 모토(酛)라 부른다. 즉, 자기 말 그대로 부른다. 그러고 보니 모두 그렇다. 코지, 모로미, 히이레, 나마자케 등.

나도 우리 술 K-Sool과 관련된 용어는 그냥 한국말로 옮기기로 했다. 누룩은 Nuruk이고 막걸리는 Makgeolli다. 밑술은 Mitsul이고 덧술은 Does-sul이다. 읽기 편하지 않을 수 있단 생각도 든다. 하지만 내 역량은 여기까지다. 조금 더 K-Sool이 알려지면 나 보다 뛰어난 더 많은 사람들이 더 나은 길을 제시해 줄 것을 믿는다.(그럼에도 불구하고, 어려운 문제가 있으면 언제든 연락해 주세요. gulekim@naver.com)

부디 많은 세계인들이 K-Sool을 접하길 바라며, 역동적인 한국 술의 세계를 즐겨 주길 기대해 본다.

How should I translate it into English?

From the moment I decided to tell my story of 'Finding My Own Nuruk,' I thought it would be great if the target audience were people from all over the world. Liquor is a universal language and has the magic of making everyone friends. I was confident that everyone who is passionate about K-Pop, K-Drama, and K-Food would welcome Korean Liquor(K-Sool).

But this hope turned into frustration as I translated the first chapter of my book. I just don't know how to translate terms related to Korean Liquor. For example, the taste and aroma of K-Sool could be deepened by growing microorganisms several times, and the first liquor brewed called '밑술(Mitsul)'. The '밑(Mit)' means 'beneath or underneath of an object,' so can be interpreted in English as 'Bottom Liquor' or 'Basement Liquor', but it is not possible to change all terms in this way or explain the meaning at every time. (Liquor added to '밑술(Mitsul)' is called '덧술(Does-sul)', and '덧(Does)' means 'repeated' or 'overlapping', so it can be called 'Repeated Liquor' or 'Overlapping Liquor' in English. Out of the frying pan into the fire.)

In that respect, the use of brewing terminology in neighboring Japan served as a good reference. In the case of Japanese sake, the base liquor is called Shubo(酒母) or Moto(酛). In other words, they call it their own words. Come to think of it, it's all like that. Koji, Moromi, Hiire, Namazake, etc.

I also decided to just translate the terms related to our K-Sool, into Korean. 누룩 is Nuruk and 막걸리 is Makgeolli. 밑술 is Mitsul and 덧술 is Does-sul. I think it may not be easy to read. But my capabilities end here. I believe that as K-Sool becomes more known, more people who are better than me will suggest a better path. (Nevertheless, if you have any difficult problems, please contact me at any time. gulekim@naver.com) I hope that many people around the world will come across K-Sool and enjoy the dynamic world of Korean Liquor.

Reason for writing this book

'Buuiju, 3/8(Tue) 2~3 days in the morning and evening'

2015 was a very difficult year for me personally.

A project that I had devoted my all to for about 2 years failed, and the company I was working for was sold to a company that I thought was inferior at the time. My colleagues were flustered and angry at the changed situation, and finally started a demo that I would never have done in my life.

I had always been busy with work for 20 years and wondered how I could reduce my workload, but once my work was gone, the pain of not having work was incomparable to the

pain of having a lot of work. I went to work, but my colleagues were outside and a few team leaders sat down and did what was necessary, but how could it have worked? And at that time, time seemed to pass so slowly. Around the time when I was mentally exhausted day by day, I happened to see a banner while riding a bus.

"Do you want to make our own Makgeolli?"

I thought it was a time when some kind of change was needed, and for me, who only had a simple concept of alcohol as a tool necessary for company dinners, the idea of making and drinking alcohol aroused strong curiosity about whether it would be possible or what it would taste like. So I went to Bundang Jinhyang K-Sool Education Center (now Balhyogosgan Dam).

The class was relatively simple. It consisted of Makgeolli and Yakju courses, and we made one predetermined K-Sool per day while listening to the characteristics of that, the meaning of recipes, and related theories during Godubap ripening or cooling. March 8, 2016 is the day when I brewed my first K-Sool, Buuiju where rice grains float. The back part says '2~3 days in the morning and evening', which seems to mean that you should stir it once in the morning and evening, but it seems that it was not written because there was no space. Still, the feeling of the words is good. '2~3 days in the morning and evening' This is how I took my first step on my long journey with my own K-Sool.

2022 Gungjungsul Brewing Competition Gold Prize

|

Unfortunately, I don't remember the taste of my first K-Sool, but I fell into K-Sool as if I were possessed by something. Starting as the 24th class of Korea Gayangju Research Institute K-Sool course at the end of 2016, I completed Distiller Master Class (DMC) and Korea traditional liquor sommelier course in 2018, Fermentation Academy Nuruk School in 2020, K-Sool course again as 36th class in 2021, and finally completed The Highest Instructor Course as 12th class in 2022. In between, twelve attempts at K-Sool competitions, two commendations, and finally won a gold medal at Gungjungsul Brewing Competition in 2022. (In other words, nine times failed.)

It wasn't passing the bar exam or being promoted to an executive position, but how happy was it on the day when I received a gold medal. And then memories of brewing alcohol while struggling passed by. On the way back on the subway where yesterday was like me but felt completely different from me. And then I wanted to organize my experiences so far. As if packing only what is necessary for a longer journey.

A book that answers questions by itself

|

William Zinsser's (1922-2015) advice also helped me write this book. He was an American writer, editor, literary critic, and teacher who wrote a wonderful book called "On Writing Well." In that book there is a question "Who are you writing for?" And since it's a fundamental problem, there's a fundamental answer. That is to say "Write for yourself." It's been eight years since I started my own journey to find alcohol by chance seeing a K-Sool brewing course banner in early spring of 2016. During that time, I brewed many K-Sool and experienced many failures and frustrations while thinking a lot.

How is K-Sool made?
What is good K-Sool?
What kind of K-Sool do I want to make?

This book is a book that answers such questions by itself. And at the center of that answer is my own Nuruk. (Fortunately, the blog I started writing in 2018 has been a great help.) Every day new K-Sool are released and more people are trying to brew K-Sool directly. If you search YouTube several times, there are plenty of ways to brew K-Sool and content overflowing with it, but actually making it easy enough is not comparable to making your own K-Sool that you really want. I am sure that my failures and experiences will be helpful to many K-Sool borrowers who have the same concerns as me.

I recommend this to those who:

- Have brewed once or twice but don't know what to do next
- Are curious about how others are brewing K-Sool
- Want to have your own unique K-Sool that doesn't exist in the world
- Even more, want to have your own unique Nuruk that doesn't exist in the world

Structure of the book

|

We could start right away with the Nuruk story, but it would be better to have some understanding of K-Sool. Parts 1-2 are for a general understanding of K-Sool. In Part 1, we try brewing K-Sool directly and organize the minimum things needed for brewing K-Sool. In particular, we focused on lowering the threshold for K-Sool brewing by placing the first articles on the ingredients and tools needed for brewing in an apartment, and the process (history) of brewing K-Sool that I have personally stepped on. In Part 2, we think about K-Sool's basic ingredients, rice, water, and Nuruk. You need to know the characteristics of each ingredient to start brewing K-Sool in earnest. And then the real Nuruk story begins.

Parts 3-4 are the highlights of this book. Who said that? Life is a tragedy when seen up close, but a comedy when seen from afar. The struggle to find my own Nuruk will be drawn pleasantly(?). We looked at various Nuruk and found out which Nuruk and method suits me. As you read the book, you might think, "Maybe I'll make Nuruk once."

Part 5 is the process of finding the color, taste, and scent of my K-Sool that suits my own Nuruk. Nuruk is important, but if it doesn't lead to K-Sool, it's just a decoration. At first, I was moved by using my Nuruk to brew my own K-Sool, but gradually I began to wonder what color, taste, and scent my alcohol would have. Rather than vaguely good K-Sool, I believe that if you distinguish it from the perspective of color, taste, and scent, K-Sool will be clearer.

Occasionally there are '※Refer to' between articles and '▶K-Sool Competition Challenge' every time a long article passes. Refer to is literally an important matter that I want to tell you in a separate article, and K-Sool Competition Challenge is a summary of my experience in various K-Sool competitions over several years. The K-Sool competition that started with a vague thought of how others would evaluate my K-Sool has grown me vividly so you can expect it.

Note

I

First of all, this book does not (of course it doesn't have the ability) provide detailed information on K-Sool recipes or brewing processes. It would be best to listen to and see regular courses such as Korea Gayangju Research Institute, Korea Traditional Liquor Research Institute, Makgeolli School for brewing K-Sool, or if that is not possible, at least Ryu In-su's <Korea traditional liquor textbook> should be placed next to it for reference.

In addition, Baegse or Chaeju or other brewing terms are all written in easy language as much as possible. But one thing is that the word Korea traditional liquor that we often use feels a bit old-fashioned. Some people call it Korea liquor and some call it K-Sool, but I decided to call it K-Sool. It's not important, but my book uses plain language. I wrote in a way that maximizes the sense of reality as if I were speaking normally, but if there are any who feel rude in advance.

Finally, before publishing the book, I received proofreading from you all to make sure there were no mistakes. Nevertheless, if it is different from what I know, it is entirely due to my lack of knowledge. Occasionally when listening to K-Sool stories, some people say 'This is this' 'That should be done like this' as if there is a definite answer. Even if you brew with the same recipe every day and night, the taste is different and Gayangju means our home liquor after all so finding liquor that suits my taste is a process so how about being generous? And that's also the charm of K-Sool.

I'd like to start with a quote from J. Krishnamurti that I usually like.

"Now forget everything you know about yourself. Forget your thoughts about yourself so far. We're going to start as if we don't know anything. It rained heavily last night and now it's starting to clear up. It's a new and fresh day. Let's meet this new day as if there's only one day left. Leave yesterday's memories behind and let's go on a journey together. And let's start understanding ourselves for the first time."

Part 1
K-Sool Brewing Challenge

Before we get into the story in earnest, let's brew some K-Sool together. A golden, glowing glass of clear, hand-brewed K-Sool will soon come to mind, but I'm sorry, we have to wash the rice first. The K-Sool you want will take at least a month to taste even if you start now. (And it may not even be the taste you were expecting.) So it's better to start lightly. You need to get used to brewing K-Sool before you have the time to taste and understand the principles.

First, let's have a glass of K-Sool

How alcohol is made

|

In the Gospel of John, Jesus performed a miracle by turning water into wine at a wedding in Cana, but even now, more than 2000 years later, when I see alcohol boiling up, it feels like a miracle.

How is alcohol made?

|

This seemingly simple question was not revealed until 1866 by Louis Pasteur, long after the microscope was invented in the 17th century. It is yeast. Yeast is a complete organism that is born, grows, reproduces, and dies, but it is too small to be seen with the naked eye. (That's why it's called a microorganism because it uses the character 'micro' to mean small.) It is not certain why yeast makes alcohol. The most credible claim is that of food scientist Choi Nak-eon.

Yeast's strategy is useful but also fatal to itself. In fact, the highest alcohol content that can be obtained from fermented liquor is theoretically 25 degrees, because it cannot withstand the alcohol it produces. Therefore, this strategy should not be used when it is good to eat and live, but when it is really hard to live. How hard? Don't be surprised. It's an environment without oxygen to breathe. (Fortunately, yeast can survive even without oxygen.)

Crush grapes @pixabay.com

In summary, alcohol is a byproduct produced by yeast in a difficult situation without oxygen (to eat and survive alone). It cannot be produced indiscriminately and requires food such as glucose, which is found in grapes and called glucose because it is a source of energy for living organisms. In fact, grapes are very rich in it, so if we crush grapes and put them in a jar and close them so that air does not pass through them, they become alcohol. (That's wine.)

There are many alcoholic beverages made from grapes in our ancient literature, but since rice is the staple food, a culture of brewing alcohol using rice has developed. It would be nice if alcohol could be made just by putting crushed rice in a jar like wine, but unfortunately, yeast has a small mouth and cannot eat large and tightly packed tissues like rice. Therefore, the starch structure of rice must be finely cut into glucose units, which is called saccharification.

Saccharification is done by enzymes, not microorganisms, and the representative saccharifying enzyme is amylase contained in our saliva. This is why rice becomes soft and sweet when we keep chewing it. So if you chew rice and spit it out and close it, it becomes alcohol. In Makoto Shinkai's 2016 feature-length animation "Your Name," the female protagonist Matsuhara makes alcohol in this way. It's called 'Kuchikamizake', which translates to 'chewing alcohol' (also called 'beauty sake').

We could chew rice hard to make and drink alcohol, but fortunately we have Nuruk. Nuruk is a treasure trove of various enzymes and yeasts. Like crushing grapes to make wine, Godubap is cooked, water is poured, and Nuruk is mixed and closed to make K-Sool. That's why the main ingredients of K-Sool are rice, water, and Nuruk.

To summarize the principle of becoming alcohol that we have talked about so far: (The starch in the rice is saccharified into glucose using enzymes produced by mold, and this is fermented by yeast to produce alcohol.)

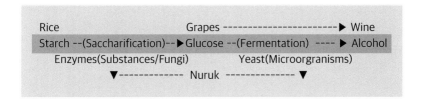

Please prepare

|

Let's actually make K-Sool. It's called 'Seogtanju', which is so delicious that it's a shame to swallow. Seogtanju, Seogtanhyang, and Hwang-geumju are all the same method of alcohol, but it was called Hwang-geumju depending on the color of the alcohol, and when it became widely known, someone named it Seogtanju. The method is simple, but sweet and soft, so many people who are brewing K-Sool for the first time challenge it.

A few preparations are needed.

Specific things like scales or ladles will be discussed in the next article, so let's just start with what we have at home for now. First of all, you need rice, water, and Nuruk mentioned earlier. Two types of rice are needed: Non-glutinous rice flour and Glutinous rice. Glutinous rice can be bought at a local mart, but Non-glutinous rice needs to be ground into flour, so it is convenient to buy 'wet salt-free Non-glutinous rice flour' on the Internet and use it. Water can be boiled tap water or purified water or bottled water. If you search for Nuruk on the Internet, there are several brands, but Songhakgokja Soyulgog seems to be used a lot because it is easy.

How much to buy is determined by considering the amount that can be worked at once at home based on the Seogtanju recipe below.(The method of writing and reading recipes is summarized in the next article 'References'.)

	Rice	Water	Nuruk	Method
Mitsul	2	10	1.2	Porridge
Deos-sul	10			Glutinous rice Godubap
	12	10		Total 22L (Container over 27L)
	1 :	0.8		10% Nuruk of the total amount of rice

It would be difficult to build Godubap 10kg at a time. If you can steam up to 2.5kg at a time with a steamer at home, you can reduce it in proportion to this amount.

	Rice	Water	Nuruk	Method
Mitsul	0.5	2.5	0.3	Porridge
Deos-sul	2.5			Glutinous rice Godubap
	3	2.5		Total 5.5L (Container over 7.2L)
	1 :	0.8		10% Nuruk of the total amount of rice

You will need 500g of wet salt-free Non-glutinous rice flour, 2.5kg of Glutinous rice, 300g of Nuruk, and 2.5L of water. If you buy a large amount at once, the remaining rice flour can be frozen and thawed for use, and Nuruk can be completely sealed and kept in a cool place out of direct sunlight, but it is best to use it immediately as its strength may decrease and bugs may occur if left for too long. For reference, if you dry Nuruk in the sun a few days before use to reduce the smell, the K-Sool will be better. (This is called Beopje, which is very important to remember.)

Shall we brew together?

Once the ingredients are ready, let's brew K-Sool together. But before that, I want to say one important thing. As you will see, it may look easy to see, but the thought and reality are very different. What container to use right away, how to make porridge, whether there is rice at home, where and how much to wash, whether there is a sieve, how Godubap and eating rice are different… Decisively, am I doing well now.

If the head goes ahead of the hand, it will definitely fail. We are dealing with living organisms now. And it's invisible to the eye. So there is a tendency, but there is no answer. There may be no answer and it may be frustrating, but there is a rather exciting side. Let's just focus on the process of making alcohol comfortably.

When brewing K-Sool becomes familiar to your hands, you naturally feel the difference in taste and become curious about the principle. Even if I tell you everything now, you won't be able to understand it. Previously, Park Rok-dam, head of the Korea Traditional Liquor Research Institute and the best Korea traditional liquor teacher in our country, released a video of brewing K-Sool with BTS Jin and Baek

Jong-won, and I was impressed when I heard the following words.

"I learned from my grandmother that if I do this, it becomes K-Sool, but if it doesn't work, there is no one to ask. When I ask, the words change from time to time. I thought they didn't want to teach me. So I wandered for 10 years. After knowing how to make K-Sool later, both what you said this way and what you said that way were right." "What is that?" "The season has changed. The season has changed between when I learned K-Sool and when I was brewing it." [2] Let's try it together for a while even though it's curious right now. There will be plenty of time for deep talk in the future.

Brewing Mitsul

What is the first thing to do when brewing K-Sool?

It is disinfection. All containers and tools are boiled or wiped with disinfectant alcohol. Pour 500g of wet salt-free Non-glutinous rice flour into a suitable bowl and add about 500ml of water and mix well. The remaining 2L of water is boiling, and when it is completely boiled, reduce the heat and pour the Non-glutinous rice flour water that was opened and cook the porridge. At this time, stir well with a ladle so that the bottom does not burn, and if you are worried about burning, you can reduce the heat very low and stir. When the porridge pops up, it's done, so cover it and put it in a cool place to cool completely. (Just leave it outside overnight.)

Mix rice flour with water (left), cook porridge in boiling water (middle), leave hot porridge outside overnight to cool (right) (※For convenience, the amount of ingredients has been increased in the picture. Please do not be mistaken.)

Add 300g of Nuruk to the cold porridge and mix well. You can use your bare hands, but don't forget to disinfect (wash your hands) before mixing. After mixing, there is no loss of one grain, so make sure there is nothing on your hands and cover it with a cloth and put it in a place where sunlight does not enter the house. If the house is too cold, it is good to wrap it with clothes or something. Let's get into the habit of washing containers or tools right away after use. More than half of brewing K-Sool is washing dishes.

Put Nuruk in cold porridge (left), mix well and wipe around (middle), cover with cloth (right)

Deciding on the Deos-sul time

|

When to do Deos-sul is one of the most important topics in the K-Sool process.(It's not that easy.) Let's see what happens as we take off the cloth in the morning and evening and stir vigorously with a scoop.

Stirring with a scoop has two effects. One is to evenly coat the enzymes. Enzymes are not living things as substances. Therefore, they cannot move on their own, so they must be well mixed separately. The other reason is to give fresh oxygen to the yeast. As the yeast increases, the alcohol mixes itself, but there may be a lack of oxygen at the bottom. Stir from the bottom to prevent sediment from settling on the floor.

First day (left), second day (middle), third day (right) (all taken after stirring)

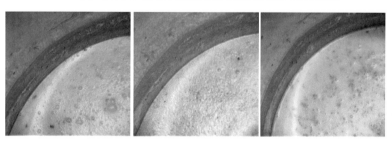

Fourth day (left), after stirring and time has passed (middle),
after stirring just before the last Deos-sul (right)
What is the biggest difference between these photos?

What is the biggest difference between these photos?

The degree of foam on the surface. Foam is created by carbon dioxide produced by yeast. Yeast initially makes alcohol to save itself, and at this time carbon dioxide and heat are generated together. The stuffy nose when you put your nose close is carbon dioxide, and the fermentation jar gets warm because of heat. Anyway, a lot of foam means that yeast is working hard. The third day photo looks like there is no foam, but it's not that there isn't any, but that saccharification has progressed so much that there isn't enough sticky stuff to make foam. If you look closely, you can see small bubbles bursting without rest. On the fourth day, bubbles exploded and even made a foam layer again. (※The actual Mitsul appearance varies depending on how it was processed and which Nuruk was used. It would be good to see it for reference only.)

Although it is not visible to the eye, yeast is diligently eating sugar and giving birth to children. One yeast gives birth to an average of 24 children, and the cycle is 2 hours. If you calculate it, the first yeast starts dying after living its entire life from 48 hours, and it doubles every 2 hours, so the first yeast increases by 2 to the 24th power, or 16,777,216.(This is called exponential…)

The best time to do Deos-sul is when there are the most yeasts. It would be best to look through a microscope, but it is not easy to judge whether it is still in a state of continuous proliferation or at its best just by looking at it. This is why you need to develop your sensory evaluation skills by brewing alcohol several times. For detailed Deos-sul timing judgment methods using all five senses such as eyes, nose, ears, mouth, etc., refer to <Korea traditional liquor textbook>, and in my case, when boiling subsides sufficiently and all wheat sprouts rise up and look like nothing happened Deos-sul.(This point is called a stationary period.)

Doing Deos-sul

|

Deos-sul begins with preparing Godubap. Measure 2.5kg of glutinous rice and wash it clean. At this time, be careful not to rub it tightly like when making rice. So that rice grains do not break as much as possible, put your hand between rice grains and rotate in one direction so that they collide with each other naturally and wash or shave off outside naturally.(It looks complicated when explained, but if you watch related YouTube once, you will understand quickly.)

When rice is washed enough, put water in and out or put it under running water so that all floating matter or broken pieces between rice grains are washed away. At first there are a lot of rice water but it gets clean faster than you think so don't worry about it. Washed rice should be soaked for at least 3 hours or more.(If you're busy, you can soak it a little longer.) In the meantime, rice absorbs water and becomes softer as it soaks for a long time, making it easier to steam. However, if left too long, various components of rice can dissolve in water and escape from alcohol can become dry so caution is needed. When you think it's time enough, carefully scoop out rice grains so they don't break and drain water for about an hour. And during that time prepare for Godubap cooking.(If you tilt the colander slightly, water will drain better.)

Godubap is similar to steaming dumplings. Boil water under a steamer and cook rice with steam from boiling water. It's convenient to proceed with matching the time for draining colander water with boiling steamer water. When steam rises in the steamer, lay a cloth on top of glutinous rice and steam for about 50 minutes from then on and let it sit for about 10 minutes.

After washing rice (left), putting it in (middle), cooking Godubap (right)

After the Godubap is done, spread it out and cool it down.(By the way, if you want to cool it down quickly, it's good to turn on a fan.) While Godubap is completely cooled, squeeze Mitsul. The reason for squeezing Mitsul is to remove the wheat sprouts contained in Nuruk. If wheat sprouts continue to be present, the color of the alcohol will darken and the taste and scent of Nuruk will impair the flavor of the alcohol. Usually, after squeezing it separately in a stand basin, it is mixed with Godubap, but in this case, since the amount was not much, it was squeezed directly into the fermentation tank.(Again, be sure to disinfect the basin, fermentation tank, and hands frequently to avoid contamination.)

Cooling Godubap (left), disinfecting fermentation tank (middle),
squeezing Mitsul (right)

Squeezing alcohol (Chaeju)

|

If you search for Seogtanju(Seogtanhyang) recipe in ancient documents, most of them say 'use after 7 days after Deos-sul', but I personally think it's short.

The question of how long it will take for alcohol to ripen is like this problem. I want to say at least 3 weeks and at most 3 months. The reason why I thought at least 3 weeks was because I saw a paper called 'A Study on the Chemical Characteristics of Cheongju by Low Temperature Fermentation' from then on. In the paper, there are experiments on fermentation period by fermentation temperature and about 20-25 days at 25 degrees, about 30-35 days at 18 degrees, and more than 50 days at 10 degrees.(Below is a capture of related papers [3])

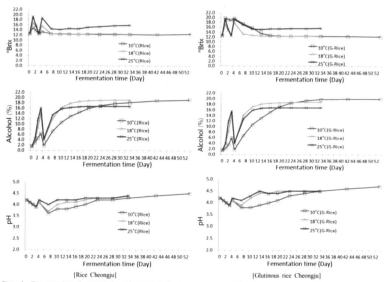

Fig. 1. Fermentation characteristics of Cheongju by temperature conditions.

To explain further, if you look at the picture above, there are graphs of sugar content(Brix), alcohol, and acidity(pH), and the result values at fermentation temperatures of 10 degrees, 18 degrees and 25 degrees depending on the color. The three graphs on the left mean Non-glutinous rice(Rice) and Glutinous rice(Glutinous rice) on the right. Overall, you can see that the measured values wobble twice in the beginning, which is a change that occurs every time Deos-sul is done and can be seen as being manufactured by Samyangju method. If you look at each item, sugar content increases when temperature is high, alcohol grows larger as temperature is lower, and acidity converges similarly over time. The fermentation period can be seen as a point where the change in alcohol has stabilized to some extent and red, light green and blue in order from red to blue match temperature difference.(In other words, a longer fermentation period is needed at low temperatures.)

> For reference, if you search for papers related to Korea traditional liquor, you will be surprised to find that there are more and more diverse than you think. If you are familiar with reading papers rather than relying on uncertain data, throw a keyword you are curious about on the Internet. You never know if an unexpected big fish will come up from time to time.

Of course, even if fermentation has not progressed enough, alcohol can be squeezed out but wouldn't it be better if it was fully ripe and deepened in taste and scent? Especially if there are no problems, taking a longer fermentation period can give rich flavors such as tropical fruit scent. However, if left for a long time at high temperature during summer or left for more than 3 months at room temperature rather than low temperature, it can smell like soy sauce, so be careful.

Seogtanju opened after 3 weeks, alcohol is solidifyin (left), 4th week, more solidified(right)

In this case, alcohol was squeezed out after one month. You can use a sieve called Siajumeoni to squeeze it out. The amount of alcohol depends on the strength of your hand grip so it may be hard but it would be good to use some strength.(It's interesting that even commercial breweries with mechanical filters prefer(?) to squeeze by hand. Alcohol comes out more or something.)

Low temperature aging

|

There is a saying that the K-Sool that has just been squeezed out has the worst taste. This expresses the charm of aging, which means that aging is important. The first squeezed alcohol is strong and rough. However, as you age in the refrigerator, it becomes softer and calmer. As time passes, the sediment settles and it is also fun to be able to drink clear alcohol separately from the top. Although your mind may be in a hurry, it is recommended to drink after leaving it in the refrigerator for a few days.

And, if you didn't do anything differently, the alcohol content of the K-Sool you made is at least 17 degrees or more. Nowadays Soju is 16.9 degrees, so you can't take a shot in a glass thinking of Makgeolli on the market. Among the recently released Makgeolli, there are advertisements that say to drink on the rocks with ice, which is a good way. However,  if you dilute water to lower the alcohol content and drink it, you must leave it for at least 3 days after watering to properly harmonize alcohol and water.

Tasting

|

Seogtanju was made for the first time in a long time while writing a book. As expected, it was very sweet and especially this time the K-Sool had a moderate sourness that followed and I liked it even more. (After thinking about it later, it seems like I used Nuruk that I didn't usually use. For reference, I used Baeksuldoga Nuruk (Jinjugokja)). It's good to enjoy alone, but it's even better with family, and if you show your line to acquaintances around you, you will be surprised at yourself brewing K-Sool while increasing the amount and losing sleep at night.

•Reference•

How to write a recipe, how to read a recipe

Measurement units

|

If you follow the original form of the K-Sool recipe, you will come across a Joseon Dynasty recipe. For example, in a book called "Sulbangmun" from the 1800s, the method of making Seogtanju is written as follows.

"Grind 2 deo of white rice into powder, pour 1 mal of boiling water and cook porridge, then cool it. Mix in 1 deo of Nuruk powder and let it sit. In spring and summer, it takes 3-4 days, and in autumn and winter, it takes 6-7 days and then wash 1 mal of rice several times and steam it until it is cooked." [4]

There are measurement units called deo and mal, and the exact volume of 1 deo is 4.9 chon x 2 chon x 2 chon in <Sejong Sillok>, which holds 570ml of water and 540g of non-glutinous rice, but since the measurement is done with the same container and the unit increases by multiples, it is enough to match the container. In other words, if you measure non-glutinous rice powder twice with any container and put it in, you can cook porridge by putting water in the

container and put it in, you can cook porridge by putting water in the same container ten times. (10 deo is 1 mal.)

Ryu In-soo, the chief header of Korea Gayangju Research Institute, also said that he didn't know this at first and kept failing to brew alcohol, but he got a hint from the ancient text saying "measure water in the container in which you measure the rice" and had no problem afterwards.(How big an event was it that the cover of <Korea traditional liquor textbook> had the phrase "쌀 된 되로 물도 돼야".)

If you make the standard for rice and water based on volume rather than weight, you can easily predict the rice:water ratio, taste according to total volume and rice:water ratio, and even predict the size of fermentation vessel needed for a four-in-one effect. Even if you use weight instead of volume as a standard, water has the same volume and weight so it doesn't matter, and rice, Nuruk, flour etc. are slightly different but if you see them as the same, brewing alcohol becomes much easier.(For example, seeing white rice 2 deo water 1 mal as white rice 2kg water 10L.)

However, if you really want to brew alcohol according to the literature, refer to the following weights per grain for 1 deo.

Raw materia	Non-glutinous rice	Glutinous rice	Nuruk	Flour	Peelde green beans	Rice barley	Brown rice	Water
Weight(g)	540	530	400	320	470	500	440	570

Finally, one thing to note is that while frequently used units such as hop, deo, and mal are correct, units such as sabal, bokja, bari, byeong, and dong may vary in ratio depending on the recipe, so it may be necessary to double-check through the ancient text DB.(See the next reference for the ancient text DB.)

Example 1

Challenge! K-Sool >

Challenge, Brewing Samyangju (Please take a look at the recipe.)

 OOO Eager member
2023.2.5 Check 246

Brewing recipe.
- Non-glutinous rice: 3.9kg - Flour: 100g -Nuruk: 400g - Water: 4L

*Mitsul: Rice flour 400g(Beonmbeog), Nuruk 400g, Water 1.6L
*Does-sul1: Rice flour 500g, Flour 100g(Gumeongtteog), Water 2L
*Does-sul2: Non-glutinous rice Godubap 3kg, Water 400g

I saw the Seoul Intangible Cultural Heritage Samhaeju Recipe and made it my own.
There, water was added during the last Does-sul2.

I'm debating whether to make Does-sul1 with Godubap or Gumeongtteog.
Ask your seniors for advice.

When writing a recipe, write rice, water, Nuruk, flour, and processing method in the order of adding stage, and finally write the total amount of rice and water and convert the rice:water ratio to predict the final taste of K-Sool. Even if you have written down a somewhat complicated process of brewing, if you write it down again like this, the process, purpose and result will be neatly organized.

Let's take an example. The capture image above is a post by someone on a K-Sool brewing site that I frequent. It looks a bit complicated but can be easily summarized.

	Rice	Water	Nuruk	Flour	Method
Mitsul	0.4	1.6	0.4		Beombeog
Deos-sul1	0.5	2		0.1	Gumeongtteog
Deos-sul2	3	0.4			Non-glutinous rice Godubap
	3.9	4.0	Total 7.9L		
	1 :	1	Nuruk 10%, Flour 25%		

If you organize the recipe, you can see the following things at a glance.

Firstly, it is Samyangju that does Deos-sul twice. Secondly, the total volume is 7.9L, so a fermentation vessel of at least 30% larger than that should be used for more than 10L. Thirdly, the rice:water ratio is 1:1, so it will be a moderately sweet K-Sool. Fourthly, Nuruk is used at 10% of the rice amount and flour at 25% of the Nuruk amount, so there seems to be no problem with saccharification and fermentation.

I just brought any article to show an example, but if you organize the recipe, you can see several strange points. First of all, both Mitsul and Deos-sul1 have a rice:water ratio of 1:4, but one is Beombeog and the other is Gumeongtteog. Usually, the processing method is Beombeog from 1:2 to 1:4, but it looks unnatural to use Gumeongtteog with the same ratio. Gumeongtteog is a processing method used when you want to use very little water compared to the amount of rice.

It also looks strange that a small amount of water is added to Non-glutinous rice Godubap in Deos-sul2. Usually, when using Non-glutinous rice for the last Deos-sul, boiling water of the same amount is poured to dissolve the rice well(called Tanghon), but there is no such thing in the above recipe, so it may be difficult to handle a large amount of Godubap that comes in at the end. Looking at the comments, it seems that someone wrote it after watching a YouTube video, but unfortunately I would like to say that it is a recipe that will not work well for K-Sool. Whether it's Korea Traditional Liquor Research Institute or Korea Gayangju Research Institute, once you listen to a regular course related to K-Sool, it's easy, but if you only want to know Samhaeju recipe, don't rely on word of mouth and use Korea liquor ancient text DB.(See next article for ancient text DB)

Example 2

Challenge! K-Sool >

I challenge my first Seogtanju

 OOO Genera member
2023.3.15   Check 128

It's the 5th day since I made my first Seogtangju because I wanted to savor the taste of K-Sool after I made and drank Danyangju regardless of the taste to drink makgeolli on a regular basis! The picture was taken the next day after Does-sul. I tried watching the Sulikneun-Jip YouTube!

Mitsul – Non-glutinous rice 500g, Water 2.5L, Nuruk 200g
Does-sul – Glutinous rice Godubap 2kg

It went like this. I tried not to open the lid, but surface seemed dry, so I mixed it once on the third day. I don't know if it will turn out well, but I'm waiting with half expectation and half worry. After making coal wine once, I got greedy, so I'm going to make a bottle of coal liquor, and next week when the ingredients come, I'm going to make Samyangju according to the recipe on YouTube.

I think I have a new hobby.

Let's take another look while we're at it.

If you write the recipe as is written, it looks like this.

	Rice	Water	Nuruk	Flour	Method
Mitsul	0.5	2.5	0.2		
Deos-sul	2				Glutinous rice Godubap
		2.5	2.5	Total 5L	
		1 :	1	Nuruk 8%	

It's a congratulatory thing to have a new hobby, but the recipe doesn't look as enjoyable.

First of all, there is no mention of Mitsul's processing method. The rice:water ratio is 1:5, so it must be 'porridge', but it would have been nice to explicitly indicate it. And the total rice:water ratio is 1:1. Seogtanju has a rice:water ratio of 1:0.8 and is a very sweet K-Sool. Maybe they wanted to reduce the sweetness on 'Sulikneun Jip' YouTube channel, but there is a unique reason why Seogtanju is called Seogtanju. Maybe the person who wrote this article will always know Seogtanju as a 1:1 ratio.

•Reference•

Korea liquor ancient text DB

Treasure house of the K-Sool original form

As the number of people brewing K-Sool increases, various K-Sool names are mentioned, but the methods and amounts of ingredients for brewing are often different and the way they are expressed is also different. In such cases, it would be very good to know exactly when that K-Sool appeared, how it was made, and what characteristics it has.

<Korea liquor ancient text DB> homepage (koreansool.kr, as of April 2023)

Fortunately, Kim Jae-hyung, director of Korea liquor literature research institute and senior at Korea Gayangju Research Institute, has compiled a total of 117 brewing K-Sool texts and made them into an internet DB, which is freely available without conditions, so it would be good to keep it close.(It is said that he devoted himself to research for 12 hours a day for 7 years to create it, and I feel awe beyond respect.)

For example, if you enter 'Hosanchun' in the search box of the ancient text DB, a total of 25 items will appear, two of which are Hosanchun mentioned in the contents of the recipe, and the remaining 23 are descriptions of K-Sool Hosanchun by document. It's amazing that there are so many Hosanchun, but you can see that there are different recipes for brewing differently depending on the region or family. You can also see a trend towards simplification from Non-glutinous rice Samyangju to Glutinous rice Iyangju over time, and you can guess that as you go to the late Joseon Dynasty, Glutinous rice was widely used as brewing skills were leveled up.

Samhaeju recipe

The story of Samhaeju came up in how to write a recipe, so let's find out the exact recipe. Go into the recipe section of the ancient text DB and select Samhaeju to find it. There are more Samhaeju than expected.(At the time of writing this book, 55 results were searched.) There are four different methods of Samhaeju in the widely known ancient text <Eumsikdimibang>, but the processing methods are different.

Gumeongtteog or Algokjuk etc. are unfamiliar methods, so if you choose an easy one among them, the third Samhaeju using Beombeog and Godubap looks good. The following is <Eumsikdimibang> Samhaeju 3 recipe.

	Rice	Water	Nuruk	Flour	Method
Mitsul	20	30	3	4.5	Beombeog(1st Haeil in January)
Deos-sul1	30	45			Beombeog(2nd Haeil in January)
Deos-sul2	50	75			Non-glutinous rice Godubap
					(3rd Haeil in January)
		100	150	Total 250L	
		1 :	1.5	Nuruk 3%, Flour 150%	

Only 100 deo of rice is used, which is equivalent to 54kg when converted into weight. The amount is huge. For reference, note that the amount of Nuruk used in Joseon Dynasty recipes is very small at 3-4%. In modern K-Sool courses, they say to use about 10% of the rice amount, but if you use only 3% by looking at only old recipes, alcohol will not work properly. This proves that Nuruk was much better than now in Joseon Dynasty, but unfortunately that technology has not been passed down until now. I'm sorry but let's disobey our ancestors' words as much as Nuruk's amount.

Brewing K-Sool in an apartment, no problem

I remember someone asking me where I brewed K-Sool and when I said I brewed it in my apartment, they were surprised and asked if that was possible. Perhaps it's because of the slightly old-fashioned image that Korean traditional liquor has. I haven't felt any inconvenience brewing in my apartment for 8 years, but I thought it might be helpful to organize a few things.

Setting the standard amount for brewing

|

Since not all brewing tools and facilities are fully equipped at home, there will always be a bottleneck if you look at them one by one.

In my case, the capacity of the Godubap steamer is 4kg, which is

the maximum amount that can be steamed at once. This is important because when making a recipe, this value becomes the standard. For example, if you are making Iyangju with a rice:water ratio of 1:1, since the amount of Deos-sul Godubap is fixed at 4kg, the amount of Mitsul naturally becomes 2kg and the amount of water becomes 6L based on the Beombeog standard of 3 times. The diagram is as follows. (For how to write and read recipes, see previous post)

	Rice	Water	Method
Mitsul	2	6	Beombeog
Deos-sul	4		Glutinous rice Godubap
	6	6	
	1 :	1	

Here, if you apply the rule that Nuruk is 10% of the total amount of rice and flour is 30% of the amount of Nuruk, the final result is as follows.

	Rice	Water	Nuruk	Flour	Method
Mitsul	2	6	600g	180g	Beombeog
Deos-sul	4				Glutinous rice Godubap
	6	6			Total 12L (Container over 16L)
	1 :	1			Nuruk 10%, Flour 30%

If you design it as Samyangju, which is called Unbeatable K-Sool, you can divide Mitsul in half.

	Rice	Water	Nuruk	Flour	Method
Mitsul	1	3	600g	180g	Beombeog
Deos-sul1	1	3			Beombeog
Deos-sul2	4				Glutinous rice Godubap
	6	6			Total 12L (Container over 16L)
	1 :	1			Nuruk 10%, Flour 30%

Preparing ingredients for brewing

|

K-Sool requires rice, water, and Nuruk. Among them, rice is used in various forms such as Tteog, Baekseolgi, Beombeog, porridge, and Godubap depending on the processing method, and all except Godubap require rice flour. Rice flour can be made by washing the rice cleanly, soaking it for more than 3 hours, draining the water for about 1 hour, and then grinding it twice without salt at a local mill. However, it is not easy from experience.

Even I, who had no reason to go to a mill in my lifetime, was no exception. It is important to choose a nearby mill and establish a relationship first. (Let's give them a bottle of homemade K-Sool. Their tone of voice will probably change.) And when you do it once, you  can put it in a zipper bag in 500g or 1kg increments and freeze it for convenience.

One thing to note is that non-glutinous rice absorbs 1.25 times water and glutinous rice absorbs 1.4 times water, increasing its weight. Therefore, if you put 1kg of rice in each bag, it means that non-glutinous rice flour should actually weigh 1.25kg and glutinous rice flour should weigh 1.4kg each, so there is no mistake.(Of course, frozen rice flour should be used after it has melted sufficiently.)

If it's cumbersome to go to the mill, you can buy wet salt-free rice flour on the internet and use it.(It seems that many people are buying and using it these days.) Until you get used to glutinous rice and start to choose varieties, you can just choose anything at the mart.(I plan to talk more about rice varieties in Part 2 'Rice, K-Sool's main ingredient and backbone of flavor.') Water should be used with tap water for convenience when washing or soaking rice, but when brewing alcohol, be sure to use purified water or boiled water that has cooled down.

Nuruk can be easily obtained on the internet. You can choose whichever is convenient for you such as Geumjeongsanseong Nuruk, Songhakgokja(Soyulgog), Jinjugokja etc., but since each Nuruk has different characteristics, it is recommended to use only one type at first to fully understand its characteristics before moving on to another one. Some people who are good at brewing K-Sool mix two or more Nuruk together, but I personally have never tried it.

One thing to note when using Nuruk is that you must expose it to sunlight and stir it for at least 2-3 days before brewing. However, if you leave it for too long, bugs will appear so if you are not using it, seal it and store it in a cool place where light does not enter.(If you see bugs that you haven't seen in your house before, Nuruk is probably the culprit!)

Preparing tools for brewing

Nowadays there are various types of stainless steel pots, strainers, ladles, fermentation tanks by capacity such as 10L distiller and 50L automatic fermenter and even 5-inch Dololara but rather than having everything from the beginning it is better to gradually increase only what is needed when needed.

I've organized only the minimum necessary things.

1) **Scale** : 'Simple Weight Electronic Scale SW-1S' from CAS seems to be the most common.(You can see this scale everywhere.) For reference, the SW-1S model is distinguished by maximum weight and measurement unit specifications. The model with a maximum weight of 30kg and a measurement unit of 10g has good value for money.

2) **Measuring cup** : Any measuring cup that can measure up to 1L in units of 100ml will do. You can also use the amount of water that comes out of the water purifier at once.

3) **Stainless steel pot** : It would be good to prepare 2-3 pots of Seonhak No.8(44cm). (There are many brands but Seonhak's products are thicker so I prefer them.) As mentioned earlier about bottlenecks in brewing alcohol since I can steam up to 4kg of Godubap at once I also proceed with washing rice based on 4kg. When using No.8 pot it is suitable for washing and especially in my case I wash rice in the bathroom so the size of the pot fits well. Pots are needed not only when washing rice but also when steaming Godubap or going to the mill.(You can reduce the size according to your own environment.)

CAS Simple Weight Electronic Scale SW-1S(left), Measuring cup also used as an electric pot when boiling water(middle), Stainless steel pots(right)

4) **Stainless steel strainer** : Used when draining water from soaked rice. It is better to choose a wide and flat one rather than a concave one so that the water drains well. When draining water, tilt it slightly.

5) **Steamer** : Used when steaming Baekseolgi or Godubap. In my case, I had a steamer at home that could steam 4kg of soaked rice at once, so I didn't have to buy one separately. From experience, the amount that can be steamed at once becomes a bottleneck in brewing, so it is important to choose carefully. Also, where to steam is also an issue to consider. Since Godubap cooks better with stronger heat, induction is better than gas range.(For more details on Maha-steamer, High Heat burner, High Output induction, etc., see Part 2 'Rice, K-Sool's main ingredient and backbone of flavor')

6) **Ladle** : Used when mixing Beombeog and transferring contents to a fermenter.

7) **Stainless steel ladle** : A ladle is needed when tasting K-Sool or scooping it out from time to time. It would be good to have two types, large and small, and it is easy to manage if the whole thing is made of stainless steel.

Flat stainless steel strainer(left), steamer(middle), ladle and various sizes of stainless steel ladles(right)

8) **Silicone cloth** : In the past, cotton cloth was used when steaming or cooling Godubap, but after using silicone cloth, I experienced a new world. It is highly recommended because it is easy to use and clean. However, cotton cloth is not unnecessary. A cloth cover is needed to cover the fermenter during alcohol fermentation to prevent contamination, so it would be good to have several considering laundry.

9) **Strainer(Siajumyeoni)** : Used when straining alcohol.

Silicone cloth(left), strainer(middle), cotton cloth(right)

10) **Fermenter** : If you want to brew above Iyangju, you need Mitsul and Deos-sul. One thing to note is that K-Sool can boil over, so there should be at least 30% extra space. Based on the Iyangju recipe explained earlier, if the amount of Mitsul is 8L, at least 11L or more is required and if the total amount of alcohol during Deos-sul is 12L, the fermenter must be at least 16L or more. At first it is good to start with a plastic container that is easy to obtain and shows the fermentation process but once you get used to it use a stainless steel food container or(if you are confident) a jar. Plastic containers have a unique smell that is not good. Stainless steel is all good but since there may be remaining polishing agents after purchase you should clean it well even if it takes effort.

11) **Funnel** : Used when putting finished alcohol into a bottle. There are probably one or two in the house.

12) **Thermomete** : There may be no immediate use but as time goes by there will be many occasions when temperature needs to be measured. A thermometer that can monitor ambient temperature and humidity must always be available and if there is a non-contact radiation thermometer that measures temperature by shooting infrared rays it will be convenient when cooling Godubap. There are also probe thermometers for measuring product temperature so refer to them.

Food container fermenter(left), funnel(middle), various thermometers(right)

There is a saying that carpenters do not blame their tools. It may mean that skill and ability are important regardless of equipment or tools but it can also be read as always thinking about how to produce the best results in the environment you are in.

For example if you think about the purpose of a fermenter any pot or steamer in your house can be used without any problem. There is no problem steaming Godubap even without silicone cloth. However once the basics are learned and prepared brewer upgrades one or two tools at just that moment their skills will increase significantly. Let's get used to it first and feel the difference in my alcohol. At some point you will feel that you really need properly made tools. It's not too late then.

Basic of basics

|

Brewing tools must always be disinfected before use and so must hands. It's not for nothing that our ancestors took baths on certain days and brewed K-Sool. Disinfection must always be done every time so keep this in mind. Therefore the most important tool to prepare lastly is ethanol for disinfection.

Boiling tools would be the most reliable but since it's cumbersome in my case I prefer ethanol for disinfection. You can buy it at large pharmacies but you can also search for disinfectant ethanol 83% online and buy it in large quantities for convenience.

Is there a royal road to brewing K-Sool?

Brewing one type of K-Sool 100 times

When I first started studying K-Sool, I heard a lot that in order to improve my skills, I had to choose one type of K-Sool and brew it at least 100 times. This is really credible, as if you keep brewing the same, the tools, methods, order, schedule, space, etc. will continue to be tuned and optimized for my environment. In other words, it becomes familiar to the hand, and as time goes on, all processes proceed naturally without having to put in any special effort.

When K-Sool no longer feels like (hard) labor, the taste and aroma become visible and seasonal changes are also detected. The question of why they are different when brewed with the same recipe naturally arouses interest in the components of K-Sool such as rice, water, Nuruk, etc., and this becomes the starting point for serious theoretical study.

At this point, I wonder if there is really anyone who has brewed one type of K-Sool 100 times? Yes! If you go to the blog(Enjoying Korea liquor) run by Kim Jae-hyung, director of the Korea liquor Literature Research Institute, you will find an article called 'The Hundredth Buuiju'. He himself is questioning whether he can now brew well, but I am confident that he can.

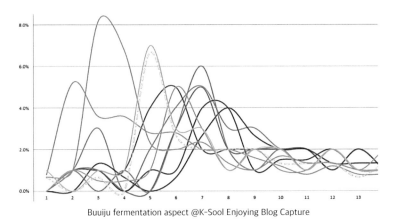

Buuiju fermentation aspect @K-Sool Enjoying Blog Capture

Which K-Sool should I start with?

The conversation has gone a little off track, so what kind of K-Sool would be good to start with? You can start with Buuiju like Director Kim Jae-hyung, but Buuiju is actually a very difficult alcohol. Instead, it seems like you can get a hint by looking around the K-Sool course practice process at the Korea Gayangju Research Institute. If you look at the content of the K-Sool course master·master class practice, you can see that the process of brewing K-Sool is designed according to the ratio of rice:water.(For reference, in the master class, Dongjeongchun, Sunhyangju, Bansengbansuk, Baeksuhwandongju, Moju etc. are learned from the literature class, except that Sunhyangju and Bansengbansuk are 1:1 ratio.)

1:1	Tteog type	→ No practice, instead Danyangju and Gwahaju are 1:1 ratio
1:2		→ Bokbunjaju
1:3	**Beombeog type**	→ **Samyangju**
1:4		→ Dangguiju
1:5	Porridge type	→ Seogtanju
Extra	Gumeongtteog	→ Ihawaju

You can see that the practice is centered on the rice water ratio and the first thing to do is 1:3 Beombeog type Samyangju. In early Joseon Dynasty there were many porridge type Mitsuls but as K-Sool making techniques developed later on Beombeog type recipes became more common. Beombeog type Mitsul comes later than porridge in Deos-sul time but yeast proliferation time is sufficient so microbial quantity increases and this leads to high alcohol content and stable fermentation. At Korea Gayangju Research Institute it is called an absolutely fail-proof K-Sool In other words, it is called an unbeatable K-Sool.

I started with Glutinous rice Iyangju using Ssias-sul. Maybe because I was burdened with doing Deos-sul twice and had a safety device called Ssias-sul that was almost(?) like Samyangju. Make Beombeog with 300g of rice and 1L of water and make Ssias-sul with Nuruk 500g(originally 600g), then divide it in half and use it for  two recipes with a total rice amount of 6kg.(I have briefly summarized Ssias-sul in the next 'See also' article.)

	Rice	Water	Nuruk	Method
Ssias-sul	0.3	1	0.5	Beombeog
Mitsul	2	6	Half Ssias-sul	Beombeog
Deos-sul	4			Glutinous rice Godubap
	6	6	Total 12L	
	1 :	1	Nuruk 4.2%	

As mentioned in the article 'Brewing K-Sool in an Apartment : No Problem', since the amount of Godubap that can be steamed at once is set at 4kg, it was arranged as above. Depending on the season, it usually takes about three days from Mitsul to Deos-sul and then steams Godubap on weekends. In other words, if you arrange Mitsul and Ssias-sul in reverse order so that Saturday is the day when you have a lot of work to do, it will be convenient.(If you do Deos-sul on Saturday, you have to do Mitsul on Wednesday, and make Ssias-sul on the previous Sunday.)

Using Ssias-sul Non-glutinous rice Iyangju

Once you get used to Glutinous rice Iyangju using Ssias-sul, you can change the ingredients. Non-glutinous rice. Non-glutinous rice is difficult to soak, so after steaming Godubap, pour the same amount of boiling water and soak for a day, taking this into account to adjust the total amount of water and adjust the Deos-sul schedule.

	Rice	Water	Nuruk	Method
Ssias-sul	0.3	1	0.5	Beombeog
Mitsul	2	2	Half Ssias-sul	Bansaengbansuk
Deos-sul	4	4		Non-glutinous rice Godubap
	6	6	Total 12L	
	1 :	1	Nuruk 4.2%	

While the rice : water ratio of 1:3 makes it very easy to make Beombeog, when the ratio changes to 1:1, it becomes difficult to fully cook the rice flour. It is called Bansengbansuk because it is half cooked, and Bansengbansuk type recipes are often used as a processing method. One thing to note is that unlike porridge or Beombeog, since the rice flour is not fully dissolved, it can boil up quite a bit. A large fermentation vessel should be used to avoid disaster.

The appearance of boiling alcohol (left), and the appearance of being greatly extinguished after stirring (right)

For Non-glutinous rice Godubap, we will look more specifically in Part 2 'Rice, K-Sool's main ingredient and backbone of flavor', but since it is not easy to cook compared to Glutinous rice, it needs to be soaked for a long time and steamed twice, and crucially after steaming Godubap, pour the same amount of boiling water and soak for a day. In other words, Non-glutinous rice Godubap for use in Deos-sul must be steamed the day before, so schedule planning is necessary taking this into account.(Personally, one of the reasons why Non-glutinous rice Godubap is good is because alcohol is not sweet, but also because there is no need to cool down after steaming Godubap.)

Iyangju, Samyangju, Oyangju
|

I had been making glutinous rice or non-glutinous rice Iyangju using Ssias-sul(of course, expe rimenting with various secondary ingredients in the middle), but I decided to change it to Samyangju when I entered the National Gayangju Brewer Selection Competition.

Most of the award-winning works are made of Samyangju, so I found out that there is a big difference in quality compared to Iyangju, and the reason is that the burden of Deos-sul once more has decreased as my material processing skills have improved. In addition, once you taste Samyangju clear liquor fermented at low temperatures in midwinter, it is hard to get out of its charm.(You'll know when you drink it, but the class is different.)

	Rice	Water	Nuruk	Method
Ssias-sul	0.3	1	0.5	Beombeog
Mitsul	1	2	Ssiassul	Beombeog
Deos-sul 1	2	4		Beombeog
Deos-sul 2	8	7		Non-glutinous rice Godubap
	11	13	Total 24L	
	1 :	1.2	Nuruk 4.5%	

At this point in my case Ichanged Nuruk to Seolhwagog.(Seolhwagog will be explained in detail in Part 4 'My Nuruk'.)

Seolhwagog is a non-glutinous rice scattered Nuruk so it must be at least Samyangju so at first I experimented with Sunhyangju method but it didn't fit my environment. Then I heard that SeoulTakju was made into Oyangju and I also officially accepted Oyangju method. Especially Oyangju includes a technique called 'Dividing Godubap' so you can change the type of rice by dividing it into two parts and also change the processing method so it is effective for making various alcohols. For detailed recipes and how to brew Oyangju alcohol refer to <Korea traditional liquor textbook>.

The following is an Oyangju recipe using Seolhwagog as Jumo. (Just for reference. Details will be explained in Part 4.)

	Rice	Water	Nuruk	Method
Jumo		3.9	2.6(Seolhwagog)	Mix(rice:water ratio 1:1.5, 6days)
Mitsul	1	2	Jumo	Beombeog
Deos-sul1	2	4		Beombeog
Deos-sul2	2	4	1(Seolhwagog)	Beombeog(Add Seolhwagog)
Deos-sul3	4			Glutinous rice Godubap
				(Dividing Godubap)
Deos-sul4	4	4		Non-glutinous rice Godubap
				(After filtering Deos-sul3)
	12	14	Total 26L	
	1 :	1.17	30% Nuruk of the total amount of rice	

Somehow, I have raised my level with Iyangju, Samyangju, and Oyangju, but it is important to understand that the essence of brewing K-Sool, such as rice flour, Beombeog, Bansengbansuk, and

Godubap, is the same. Here, with changes in Nuruk, changes in main ingredients(rice), changes in processing methods, presence of sub-ingredients, and changes in temperature according to the season, colorful K-Sool comes out.

In search of new K-Sool

If you go to the K-Sool brewing cafe, there are people who are sorry that they don't have K-Sool to drink every time, but if you steam 4kg of Godubap at a time and add various experiments, your house will always be overflowing with alcohol. But no matter how good it is, it gets boring.

As time goes by, I naturally seem to be looking for something new and fresh. I am also stimulated by various recipes and articles on the Internet cafe and there are many K-Sools that I am interested in studying literature.

Recently, young brewers have been expanding their K-Sool horizons by getting ideas from hidden literature and interpreting them in a modern way to brew.

In my case, recently I saw a book called 'The Story

of K-Sool by Joseon Chef Seo Yu-gu', which restored 33 K-Sools from Jeongjoji's Imwonkyeongjeji and described the process and inspiration of modernizing 17 of them. I felt like I wanted to follow along and brew it. Rather than seeing K-Sool as a means of consumption, once you get used to it to some extent, why not step into a new world where you can find your own new K-Sool and never know the end.

Ssias-sul

Ssias-sul is a method devised by Director Ryu In-soo of the Korea Gayangju Research Institute to brew 'Mitsul that does not fail'.

It helps to stabilize the fermentation of Mitsul by putting twice as much Nuruk as rice in Non-glutin ous rice flour Beombeog and pre-growing wild yeast and lactic acid bacteria, and using it instead of Nuruk. In addition, normally 10% of the amount of rice should be added to Nuruk, but

with Ssias-sul, 5-6% is enough, so it is economical and produces good quality alcohol with less Nuruk smell.(The alcohol content is also 1-2 degrees higher.)

Recipe
|

The following is the standard recipe for Ssias-sul, and the amount of alcohol that can be brewed with this much is 10-12kg of rice, so the rest can be stored in the refrigerator and used.

	Rice	Water	Nuruk	Method
Ssias-sul	0.3	1	0.6	Beombeog (Non-glutinous rice)

In my case, I started with Glutinous rice Iyangju, and at this time, Ssias-sul was made by reducing Nuruk to 500g, and since the total amount of rice was 6kg, I used only half and stored the rest in the refrigerator or divided it for use while brewing other types of alcohol at the same time.(I remember that there was no problem with refrigeration for up to a month, but of course it should not be left for too long.)

How will others evaluate my K-Sool?

At some point, when you brew K-Sool to a certain extent, you become curious about how others will evaluate your K-Sool. It started with my company tasting group, but the reason for starting the group was after hearing advice from Representative Lee Han-sang of Pungjeongsa-gye at a K-Sool exhibition one year.

At first, I didn't know much, so I went around each brewery and asked questions. It's not like I asked anything special, it was things like how did you grind the rice, how did this taste come out, what kind of Nuruk did you use. While I was asking around excitedly, Representative Lee Han-sang turned to me and said this.

"It's no use going around asking like that. First of all, the K-Sool you want to brew must be clear and its taste and aroma must be refined by continuously exchanging opinions with a small number of people."

It took 10 years to make Pungjeongsa-gye Yakju, and it was so embarrassing to have played with light lips. So I gathered close acquaintances and created an company tasting group.

They were originally people who liked alcohol, and since they provided unlimited(!) alcohol, the group was quickly activated. And gradually, I received tasting evaluations for my different K-Sools in this way, which was really amazing. (I'm on the far left in the picture on the below.)

In a word, it's different for everyone. There were big trends, but the reason why everyone had different favorite K-Sools and reasons and standards was because they were all different. For example, although it's been a long time ago, I once took 5 of my K-Sools and asked 4 people to rank their favorite (1st place) and not-so-favorite (5th place).

Taster	1st K-Sool	2nd K-Sool	3rd K-Sool	4th K-Sool	5th K-Sool
Park	Good blance(1st place)	Dislike sourness(5th place)	Body, bitterness	Just sweet taste	String scent dislike
Ahn	Bland(5th place)	Thick Cheongha, taste of adding fruit wine	Original Cheongju(1st place)	Too sweet	Watery ginseng wine
Lee	Sweetness is excessive	Bitter(5th place)	Sweetness is excessive	No comment	Taste of childhood(1st place)

	Sweet	Medium sourness, moderate sweetness	Pleasant acidity, pairing important(1st place)	Too sweet	Messy taste(5th place)

The results written on the blog at the time are summarized in the table below. Particularly for the 4th K-Sool, everyone said it was sweet and it was neither 1st nor 5th place, but it was understood that it was a 1:0.9 ratio Glutinous rice alcohol. However, Park chose the 1st, Ahn and Yu chose the 3rd, and Lee chose the 5th as their respective 1st place. If forced to say, the 3rd K-Sool could be considered a more popular(?), but since the same K-Sool is mixed with both 1st and 5th place, it is actually meaningless to find out which is good. It's so divided in likes and dislikes... The tasting group continued, but I needed another way to objectively evaluate my K-Sool.

K-Sool selection contest

There used to be a TV program called 'I Am a Singer (Na-ga-su)'. Usually singers evaluate ordinary people, but in Na-ga-su, ordinary people evaluate famous singers, causing a sensation. Like who would win if Mazinger Z and Taekwon V fought. A similar thing happened in the world of Korea traditional liquor in 2010. The Gayangju competition with 91 participants was held at Seoul COEX on a national scale. This is the beginning of the current National Gayangju Brewer Selection Competition.

f you look at an article written by Heo Si-myeong, the principal of Makgeolli School who participated as a judge at the time, in Kyunghyang Shinmun, "When I opened the lid of the round of 16, unexpected results came out. Small brewery operators, alcohol teachers who have been brewing and lecturing for over 10 years, and academic factions who have taken all the K-Sool courses available in Korea fell one after another. As a judge who participated, it was an embarrassing thing." [5] He expressed his thoughts. There are several factors that he pointed out, but if you look at the interview content of Representative Ahn Dam-yoon of Na-ol-dam Brewery who received the 1st prize at that time, you can guess why.

"After making each ratio slightly different and creating a total of 30 candidate groups, we compressed them into four finalists. And when these were tasted directly by 16 acquaintances, one was finally selected.(Alcohol

12%, Brix 13, acidity 3.7) This Makgeolli was made to match the nature of the competition as much as possible. In other words, I found a taste that the public would like." It is a passage where Principal Heo Si-myeong's comment that it is not a competition to 'select artisans' but a competition to 'select K-Sool' is understood. And this is exactly what I wanted.

K-Sool competition appearance

In 2019, I applied for participation in the 10th National Gayangju Brewer Selection Competition without thinking. But by chance, the theme of the 10th competition was 100% Non-glutinous rice K-Sool. I had to receive 10kg of Gyeonggi rice Cham-Dream and submit 6L of clear K-Sool, but no matter how hard I tried, only 5L of Cheongju floated up. Looking back now, it was because I couldn't handle Non-glutinous rice properly at that time, but at that time I thought that if I just filtered well somehow, I would run around in all directions and eventually fail to submit.

Looking at my blog while writing this book, I expected 'dry and clean high-quality Cheongju with its own flavor of grain', but when I look at my tasting evaluation, it says 'bitter. Alcohol feels strong. Wheat Nuruk taste and scent follow', so it seems like it was already ruined.

From 2020 onwards, I decided to prepare for competitions more systematically. First of all, I had to decide which competition to aim for. In the first half of Gangneung Danohje Korea Changpoju Selection Competition(Lunar May 5th Danoh), in the second half Yeoju Five Grain Brewed Gayangju Evaluation Contest(October), National Gayangju Brewer Selection Competition (October), Korea Myungju Competition(November), Korea Gayangju Research Institute Gungjungsul Competition(November), etc., caught my eye.(By the way, there is a rare 'Changwon Korea traditional liquor competition (April)' held in Changwon province. It was the second competition in 2023.)

Every time I finished a big story, I added one entry story for each competition. At first, it started with a simple thought of how people would evaluate my K-Sool, but participating in K-Sool competitions made me think a lot about what kind of K-Sool people like, how to brew my target, why I failed or why I won an award. And while doing so, I feel like I've grown tremendously so I hope those who read this article will definitely try it once.

Part 2

K-Sool Basic Ingredients

In Part 1, we brewed K-Sool together and learned about the preparations and considerations for brewing at home. And through the process of brewing K-Sool that I have walked through, I don't know if those who have read this article have roughly drawn their own direction for brewing K-Sool. In Part 2, we will examine each of the basic ingredients of K-Sool, rice, water, and Nuruk. The basics must be strong to not fall over.

Rice,
the main ingredient of K-Sool and
the backbone of flavor

The main ingredient of K-Sool

|

K-Sool is commonly made with rice, water, and Nuruk. Among them, rice is the main raw material for K-Sool and a factor that determines the basic flavor. It's an old story, but Baesangmyeon Brewery once released 'My Hometown Makgeolli 8 Types' using rice produced in 8 provinces nationwide. Only the rice production area and type were different, and Makgeolli was brewed using the same manufacturing method, but the taste was greatly different6. For example, Makgeolli made with Pocheon Chucheong rice had the highest sweetness, and Gangchang Onnuri rice had the lowest, with an average score difference of 15%. There are also Makgeolli with a distinctive sour taste, or those with an apple scent or excellent clarity, so it can be said that K-Sool has 'terroir' in each region.

Which rice to use has recently become an important concern and marketing point for breweries. Han-gang Brewery, famous for Naru

Saeng Makgeolli, uses Seoul Gyeongbokgung rice(I didn't even know that rice grows in Seoul), 88-year-old bosses make Palpal Makgeolli with Gimpo Geum rice, Sejong Daewang Eoju Jang Hee-do won the President's Award with Cheongwon Saengmyeong rice, Chuyeon-dang representing Yeoju uses Daewangnim-pyo Yeoju rice, Songdo-hyang Korea traditional liquor brewery known for Samyangchun uses Ganghwa Island rice to reveal their own identity of their K-Sool.

Non-glutinous rice K-Sool, it doesn't work
|

However, if you are just starting to brew K-Sool, you don't have time to worry about the variety of rice. Mitsul uses milled or wet-salted Nonglutinous rice flour and Deos-sul usually uses Glutinous rice. The variety is usually 'mixed', so you can't tell the difference. Looking back, I learned about rice at the beginning of the K-Sool Education, but there was no urgency as to why it was rice, so I pushed it aside like other classes when I heard it even though I understood it.(That was me.)

The opportunity to seriously think about rice again comes after a problem occurs. When Ssias-sul using Non-glutinous rice Mitsul and Glutinous rice Deos-sul Iyangju become somewhat familiar, complaints(?) such as 'it is too sweet' and 'monotonous' from people around me become familiar.

It's time to change the main ingredients. To make a more lively and dry alcohol, Non-glutinous rice must be used, but it is confusing which variety to use and how to handle the ingredients. Even

Unsoaked Non-glutinous rice grain

if I do it as usual, clear alcohol does not float up or it is too difficult to squeeze(if alcohol does not flow smoothly at once, something is wrong.)

Sometimes when unsoaked grains are touched, I think this is not it. I visited Ryu In-su and said that Non-glutinous rice K-Sool, it doesn't work.

He said indifferently "Non-glutinous rice should be steamed twice and soaked in the same amount of boiling water for a day." When I said that there was no such thing when I took clas ses, he said that he talked about it in class 3 of Myungju class. There's no way… …When I looked up my class notes, it wasn't that there was a circle around that sentence! Without any basics… …I laughed shyly.

Two things to know about rice

|

One is that Glutinous rice is opaque. Glutinous rice changed even Gayangju culture during the Joseon Dynasty. If you compare Joseon documents such as Sanga Yorok(1450s) and Eumsik Dimibang(1670s), you can see that the proportion of Glutinous Rice alcohol  has increased by more than 15% and Glutinous Rice use has become widespread.7 This change also simplified the method of making K-Sool and has influenced until now.(There is a reason why many people use it.)

Compared to Glutinous Rice, Non-glutinous Rice is hard and difficult to brew. Therefore, another thing to know is how to steam Non-glutinous Rice Godubap. I summarized it in four ways.

First, soak for a long time. Soak for at least 10 hours or more. Second, cook for a long time and make sure it is cooked thoroughly. Cook for 1 hour, sprinkle with cold water and mix, then cook for another 20 minutes in two batches. Third, pour the same amount of boiling water into the cooked Godubap and let it soak for a day. One thing to note is that additional water is added to the Godubap, so you need to adjust the amount of Mitsul water in advance. Finally, use Non-glutinous rice with stickiness. The degree of stickiness can be known by the amylose content, and you can search the internet for the amylose content by rice variety. The Korea Gayangju Research Institute recommends Samgwangmi, which has a low protein content and a high amylose content. If you can handle Non-glutinous rice well, the K-Sool brewing spectrum becomes very wide. Personally, I think it's the first hurdle that must be overcome in the early stages of brewing.

The world of mixed grains

Once you have some confidence in Non-glutinous rice handling, you become interested in mixed grains. What kind of K-Sool will unpolished brown rice become? Will barley rice also produce a savory K-Sool? What happens if you brew with black rice, which contains more than four times as much anthocyanin as black beans, which is good for your health? Will it come out like Gorangju if made with millet?

I had many questions myself, but initially failed most of the time. Looking at the ingredient table alone, I wondered why it didn't work

well even though the amylose content was high. When I asked Park Seon-young, head of Guksoondang, he replied, "Starch is a difficult item. It is difficult to define clearly because the types and characteristics are so diverse.(Middle omitted) Therefore, it is difficult to talk about the characteristics of starch only by simple amylose content or amylopectin content." I asked a deeper question and found out three important points.

First, there is something called 'gelatinization temperature' in starch characteristics, and the higher this is, the higher temperature is required for gelatinization. For example, corn with a gelatinization temperature of 86.5 degrees is more difficult to gelatinize than rice with 63.6 degrees. The gas range used at home usually belongs to the weak firepower side. You need to use an induction or high-power burner that is higher than that. If you want to cook a large amount at once, it is advisable to consider using a Mahachimki from Daechang Stainless Steel Industry like the one at Korea Gayangju Research Institute. As far as I know, it costs about 1.3 million won and is 220V, single-phase and 3KW, so it can be used enough at home.(However, use a power cord line of 15A or more) (※Update: There are also high-output inductions. It is advertised as an induction for business use, but it seems to be available at home with 3.3KW 15A.)

Secondly, starch characteristics assume that there is no outer skin(dietary fiber) of the material. This was the main reason why I kept failing. Brown rice, black rice and millet are all surrounded by strong outer skin and enzymes cannot break down dietary fiber by default. So there's no way it can be alcohol. You must break down the material and bring out the starch from outside. In other words, you have to use powder.

Millet with its outer skin intact is seen

Which rice to use

Many breweries use specially named rice, but the conditions for regional specialty liquor licenses may only allow the use of agricultural products from within or adjacent regions, so restrictions may be large. Rather than planning the identity of K-Sool by choosing rice and matching the characteristics of breweries to short choices, it seems that they did not fit into short choices due to restrictions on agricultural product use depending on license type. However, it is different if it is a small-scale liquor license. There are no restrictions on agricultural product use, so any rice from all over the country can be used. For example, Seoul Brewery SeoulMakgeolli uses Chungbuk Boeun Non-glutinous rice and Jeonbuk Gimje Glutinous rice.

In general, if we look at the flow of choosing rice, it seems most important to experience various rices in Gayangju stage, find rice that suits my taste and alcohol, make efforts while adjusting strategy according to license type. In my case, I use Samgwangmi for Non-

Rice piled up in the living room

glutinous rice but I don't care about region, but after experiencing 'Asan Clear Rice Samgwangmi' through Gayangju Brewery Competition, brewing became easier and result was good so I have been using it ever since. If I start a small-scale brewery, I will continue to use it, but if it is a regional specialty liquor license, I will have to set up a brewery in Asan city or nearby cities and counties, which is realistically difficult. (Glutinous rice is not yet using a special brand, but Ryu In-su research director uses Gimje Glutinous rice and Kim Je-hyung research director likes to use Yuga Glutinous rice.)

Rather than finding small differences with similar recipes, it seems much better to bring different overall flavors of alcohol by using 100% Nonglutinous rice, 100% Glutinous rice, 1:2 or 2:1 ratio or appropriate mixed grains.

For example, Glutinous rice K-Sool usually has a strong sweetness and viscosity that divides likes and dislikes, but when Mitsul and Deos-sul are both made with Glutinous rice, gelatinization is very easy and water volume control is flexible so unique recipe composition is possible. When I actually brewed, Cheongju came out a lot and the throat was smooth and decisively impressed by the peach scent.

Rice piled up in the living room
(father-in-law mother-in-law thank you~)

Water,
K-Sool taste is water taste,
but it's an old saying

Let's talk about one of the stories floating around on the internet. There is a story that the reason why we feel Soju well or not is because of the taste of the water source where the Soju factory is located. For example, in the case of Chamisul Soju, there are three factories, each called F1, F2, and F3. F1 in Icheon, Gyeonggi-do has a sweet taste, F2 in Cheongju, Chungbuk has a bitter taste, and F3 in Iksan, Jeonbuk has a slightly bitter taste. As a result, when you drink Soju made by F1, you feel that you are drinking well, but when you drink Soju made by F2, you feel that you are not… I haven't done any experiments or anything like that, but it's a credible story. Because if the alcohol content of Soju is 17 degrees, it means that 83% of it is water, so it can be seen that the taste of water is the taste of Soju.

Only rice, water, Nuruk

|

Nowadays, there are so many different K-Sools being released that we hear less about it, but when I first learned about K-Sool, I heard a lot about how it was brewed only with rice, water and Nuruk. (If you go to the K-Sool Festival, about 7 out of 10 booths will introduce it first.)

2018 K-Sool Festival

Is there anything that is not important? Among rice, water and Nuruk, water seems to be relatively less important because it can be easily obtained from the surroundings and it is difficult to feel the difference in ingredients. However, water is an essential element for human survival and therefore a topic of interest to many people. There is even a water sommelier like a wine sommelier and Korea's first water sommelier was born in 2011. In addition, the Korean Water Sommelier Association was established in 2019 and conducts regular education and qualification exams at a level that is surprising. So what kind of water should be used when brewing K-Sool?

Water good for brewing K-Sool

Water good for brewing should have no three things. It should have no color, no smell and no special taste. It may seem like all the water in the world has no three things when you hear and see it, but in reality the taste of water varies from region to region and if you expand globally the difference in taste of water is huge. In addition, different water components affect microbial growth and greatly affect the final quality of K-Sool so water for brewing should be carefully selected.

Our ancestors showed wisdom in carefully selecting water to brew good K-Sool by reflecting specific seasons such as Cheongmyeongsu/ Gog-usu and dew-collected water such as Chulobaeg/Jeonghwasu in addition to basic guidelines such as 'always use boiled and cooled water'. In addition to this there are  many different names for water such as east-flowing water(Dongyu-su), central river water(Gangsim-su), rock gap water(Seokcheon), eaves-end flowing water(Okyu-su), plum rainwater(Maeu-su) etc. which are so finely divided that our ancestors' naming sense seems to be felt.

Once I heard about 'Baekbitang' at an internet cafe I often go to. Baekbitang is one of 33 types of water recorded in Donguibogam and it means boiling and cooling water 100 times. This breaks down the water molecules into small pieces making absorption faster and facilitating communication between meridians... I don't know. I searched for Baekbitang in actual Joseonwangjosillok.

It really comes out! "Yeongjo Sillok Volume 127 Yeongjo 52nd year March 3rd Gapsool 9th article /The king's illness worsens." It seems like just before King Yeongjo die there was a phrase saying to boil Tangje but drink Baekbitang first. The person who introduced Baekbitang actually used it for brewing and said that the taste of K-Sool generally becomes sweeter and gives umami but still boiling and cooling 100 times seems a bit…

Chulobaeg or Dongyu-su would be good

It would be great if we could brew with autumn dew but natural environment is not as good as before and there may be people who live with only true-dew(Chamisul, Korea popular Soju) alone but it will be impossible to collect enough dew to brew K-Sool. Instead if you boil tap water(called Tangsu) according to Jang Gye-hyang's grandmother's words in <Umsikdimibang> there will be no problem but boiling water every time is not an easy task.

In my opinion, the easiest way to get water for brewing would be from a water purifier. Most households have one, so it's easy to use and if it's a rental type, it's regularly maintained so there's no worry about water quality deteriorating.

In my case, in normal situations, I use water from a water purifier and in important cases such as when making a singer or when soaking special ingredients, I buy and use bottled water.

Which bottled water is good?

|

In the past, there were only a few brands of bottled water, but recently the classification has increased with deep sea water, underground saltwater, carbonated water, etc. and even imported bottled water has been imported, so the range of choices has become very large.(It's not easy to choose.) Fortunately, as mentioned earlier, the Korean Water Sommelier Association holds an annual bottled water evaluation test on World Water Day(March 22) and the results are reported through the media so you can refer to it and choose the right water for you.

Looking at the results of this year(2022), domestic deep-sea water 'Thousand Year Kids Water' took first place overall, and 'Jirisansu' took first place as domestic bottled water.(Water purifier water taste evaluation has also been added since 2018, so if you are interested, please search) I usually use Jeju Samdasu, but it is always ranked at the top and is always available at the local mart when busy, so it has good accessibility.

What about deep sea water or carbonated water?

|

As we talk about water, one thing that might come to mind is that deep sea water won first place overall in the bottled water evaluation test. What would happen if we brewed K-Sool with deep sea water?

I haven't personally experimented with it but deep sea water contains a lot of minerals such as sodium magnesium calcium which can help microbial growth but most substances are included in rice Nuruk etc. so it seems difficult to see them as necessary elements. In addition even small amounts of iron or copper can have a negative impact on alcohol so there is no need to spend expensive money on deep sea water. Carbonated water can also be seen in the same context but carbonation

Part 2. K-Sool Basic Ingredients 87 is unlikely to be maintained during brewing and carbon dioxide is naturally generated during fermentation creating natural carbonation so using carbonated water for carbonation purposes does not seem very effective.

Tap Water

I once read an article written by Kim Taek-sang Myung-in of Samhae Soju who has now deceased. The gist was that the best water for brewing Samhae Soju is natural bedrock reservoir but since it cannot be obtained in urban areas tap water is used but since it was not stated whether filtration was used or not there was room for misunderstanding.(Maybe because the contributor was Korea Water Resources Corporation?)

Tap water is safe but basically sterilized and not suitable for microbial growth. It can be used for small-scale brewing at home or for washing rice but when doing large-scale it must be filtered or softened to remove chlorine before use.

Nuruk,
a motif that brings out
the passion for exploration

K-Sool 18th grade

|

In Baduk, there are amateurs and professionals, and amateurs start at 30th grade, but if you say you can play Baduk, you are considered 18th grade and those below that are people who don't know what Baduk is and play it. There may be some differences in degree, but it's just a level of knowing how to surround your opponent and eat stones. If we rank experts who operate breweries as professionals and people like me who brew as a hobby(amateur), K-Sool 18th grade would probably be able to explain what Nuruk is and know that the taste of K-Sool changes when Nuruk changes.

Ready-made Nuruk

|

At first, like everyone else, I bought Nuruk and used it. The interesting thing is that every place where I studied K-Sool had

different preferred Nuruk. Jinhyang K-Sool Education Center(now Balhyogosgan Dam) used Jinjugokja, Korea Gayangju Research Institute used Geumjeongsanseong Nuruk, and my colleagues around me seemed to prefer Songhakgokja(Soyulgog). Recently Hanyoungseok-nuruk has been very popular.

I mainly used Geumjeongsanseong Nuruk because I learned from it, but I found out why the research institute mainly used that Nuruk after a while. If you try it, each Nuruk has a different fermentation pattern. Geumjeongsanseong Nuruk ferments faster than other Nuruk and fits well with the lecture schedule that takes place twice a week so it was chosen.(K-Sool 18th grade is not easy.)

In the early days of brewing, I focused on reducing the amount of Nuruk.(If you reduce the amount of Nuruk, the so-called Nuruk taste decreases and you can bring out the original taste and aroma of the ingredients.) Usually in the case of Iyangju, about 10% is used compared to the amount of rice but when I learned Ssias-sul I lowered it to 5% and later experimented with 4% and 3% but 4% was the best. If you look at old documents from the Joseon Dynasty, the amount of Nuruk used is about 3% compared to the amount of rice so if you want to brew alcohol with about 3% Nuruk compared to the amount of rice you need to completely change the quality of Nuruk itself.(For more information on Ssias-sul see Part 1 'Ssias-sul')

I also did experiments to check the difference between ready-made Nuruk. I mainly used Geumjeongsanseong Nuruk but also tried brewing alcohol with various Nuruk such as Jinjugokja Songhakgokja

Jeongcheolgi Nuruk Baeggeumdo MilNuruk/Ihwagog etc. but at that time my ability to properly see the state of K-Sool was lacking so it did not lead to deep learning. For example in my blog comparing Sansungnuruk vs Jinjugokja in April 2019 there is this expression about Jinjugokja Ssias-sul.

"The color is a little lighter and the smell is savory but cutting off seems more gentle fermentation power seems weaker than Sansungnuruk"

Don't make a brewery without your own Nuruk

The decisive factor that changed my thoughts and direction about Nuruk was Ryu In-soo's words(which is also the subtitle of this book) 'Don't make a brewery without your own Nuruk'. Director Ryu repeatedly emphasized that ready-made Nuruk is not for Gayangju and that having the same Nuruk ultimately leads to similar tastes and aromas so if you want your own taste and aroma i.e. your own alcohol you must have your own Nuruk.

For example how about explaining it like this?

If I said 'I wish my K-Sool was light and clean but had a unique aroma'. Usually wheat Nuruk has a large body feel while rice Nuruk has a small body feel but has a sweet taste while wheat flour Nuruk is light and light but has almost no taste or aroma but if you put raw mung beans in it it gives a clean taste and if you put cooked mung beans in it it gives a strong aroma. So if I want light clean K-Sool with a unique aroma I can use wheat flour mixed with raw mung beans and include barley which gives a unique taste and aroma in my Nuruk then even without using special ingredients or adding aroma my K-Sool will already have those characteristics.

Representative Lee Han-sang of K-Sool Pungjeongsa-gye, a representative of K-Sool, also said, 'The taste of K-Sool is determined by Nuruk, and I must have my own Nuruk to have my own K-Sool,' and '(In the end) K-Sool is a game of Nuruk,' said Park Rok-dam, director of the Korea Traditional Liquor Research Institute, so I decided to make and use my own Nuruk to brew my own K-Sool.

Making Nuruk in the 4th class of Myungju

The K-Sool brewing process at the Korea Gayangju Research Institute is a 3-month process and the first month is Myungju.

Among them, the 4th class is making Nuruk, so Nuruk is placed at the beginning of the entire process and is usually learned when you are unfamiliar and inexperienced. Looking back, there was no major difficulty in making Nuruk. At the time, the director also emphasized that 'there is no recipe', 'understanding comes first', 'you must be able to adapt to the environment and do by judgment', but it flowed in one ear and easily flowed out the other.

Instead, some keywords remained such as moisture content and particle size are important and after stepping firmly according to the 777 rule put it in styrofoam and make it. In fact, when it was made like that, Nuruk worked very well and just in case I used 6% of the total amount of rice but in two weeks all the rice became watery showing tremendous power.

For reference, the 777 rule is a method of brewing Nuruk divided into 7 days each with the first 7 days maintaining moisture microbial activation and proliferation the second 7 days releasing moisture preventing rotting and allowing hyphae to go inside and the third 7 days drying improving storage etc [8]. Again for details see <Korea traditional liquor textbook>.

Rushing blindly

|

  Although it was Nuruk made during class with unfounded confidence(?) in making Nuruk I finally caught fire with enthusiasm that I could make and use Nuruk myself. I bought coarsely ground whole wheat flour on the internet (I was surprised because it was more expensive than I thought) and prepared a Nuruk mold dew leaves and pine needles. As I learned I poured water 350ml while turning whole wheat flour 1kg mixed well then squeezed it with my hand to maintain its shape and when cut it split neatly with threads sticking out… but this couldn't happen at all.(The reason why molding didn't work is in Part 3… I thought there might not be enough water so I poured more water and ended up adding another 100ml. Somehow it took shape wrapped in dew leaves then put pine needles on a styrofoam box and put Nuruk in. According to the 777 rule microbial activation should occur during the first 7 days but my blog says this so you can see how regretful I was at that time.

"4/18.

I have no idea what's going on. The styrofoam is damp and white mold is inside out. Nuruk is pressed down and there seems to be too much moisture so I tied a rope around it and started hanging it on the veranda."

I had heard somewhere so I took it out of the box put it in a sieve and hung it on the veranda… When I opened it again I saw a well-rotted(!) Nuruk covered with white spotted mold. If you look at research institute cafes or YouTube some people seem to be loose but Huangguo fungus blooms etc. Dew leaves are really good etc. Medal only put on but Nuruk floated well etc. There are stories but why does everyone else do well but only me feel frustrated.

There's no law saying you have to die

In the meantime I saw one eye-opening advertisement.

"Fermentation Academy Center - Traditional Nuruk School 8th Opening"

And the lecture goal written on the homepage was like a ray of bright light in despair.

"For those who want to approach traditional Nuruk for the first time or systematically based on the theoretical principles of Nuruk manufacturing we will learn how to actually shape and ferment throug practice. Interpreting the fermentation principles of open-type Nuruk which is a representative Nuruk manufacturing method of Korea traditional liquor during its heyday in Joseon Dynasty modernly acquire basic skills and apply them in practical field.""

Again I thought that this world was worth living.

Gangneung Danoje Festival
Korean Changpoju Contest, 2020~2021

As part of the Gangneung Danoje Festival, the Korean Changpoju Contest has been held since 2013. According to an old article, it seems that the competition has been conducted as a Changpoju theme since 2016, when Seokchangpo began to be divided. I have been participating every year since 2020, and it is a first-half competition with plenty of time, and no other ingredients can be used except for Seokchangpo, so it is perfect for improving K-Sool skills. When I look at the recruitment guidelines, there is a unique item that says to submit it by matching the alcohol content to 12 degrees, and if you match it, additional points will be given. (It disappeared from 2020.) I remember calling the organizer directly to find out why, and I heard that they tried to increase the discrimination by matching the alcohol content of the entries, and although the additional

point system disappeared, the judges prefer that degree of alcohol content.(I remembered the taste that Representative Andam Yun's public would like and an alcohol content of 12 degrees.)

In the first year, like others, I used water boiled with Mitsul and Deos-sul for Changpo, and steamed Changpo together when I was making Godubap, but the taste and aroma of the finished K-Sool were not very characteristic. Changpo may have helped fermentation, but it flew away during the process of becoming alcohol. In addition, when I sang according to the words that I prefer 12 degrees, it became even weaker. If you look at the text written on my blog before submission, I am trying to win my mind in my own way, but it would have been difficult to win from the beginning.

"It turned out drier than I thought. The taste and aroma of Seokchangpo are very weakly expressed. It is thought that dry and faint would be better than thick and sweet."

In the second year, Changpoju Yakju came out as a guideline, and in order to make up for the failure of the first year, I tried to imprint Changpo as much as possible as a sub-ingredient. First of all, I set up a base with a rice-to-water ratio of 1:0.8 to make it sweet, and repeated my worries about whether there was a more effective way to include basic tasks such as boiling water with Changpo and steaming together with Godubap. While doing so, I got a hint from <Yangjubang> Changpyeongsul during a K-Sool course owner class that I was listening to at that time.

There are three types of Changpyeongsul in Yangjubang: one method is to extract juice and use it, and another method is to cut it into slices or slices and soak it. However, it is not put in during fermentation but added to finished alcohol. In spring or summer, it is said to be lifted in seven days and eaten hot. Later on when I learned about Hwayangipjubeop or Jujungjiyakbeop, the key point of putting in fragrance is 'putting or putting for three days before Chaeju', but if you leave it for seven days like Yangjubang... Maybe at that time judges almost received K-Sool at the level of Han Yakjae. The second challenge also failed.

Gangneung Danoje Festival
Korean Changpoju Contest, 2022

Gangneung Danoje Korean Changpoju Contest, 2022 | In my third year(2022), taking lessons from two previous failures as lessons, I aimed for balance in K-Sool. The boiling water or steaming together with Godubap that had no great effect was removed and focused on balancing fragrance through proper soaking. However, since K-Sool is not only necessary for fragrance but also requires good quality of base K-Sool itself, fortunately Seolhwagog succeeded in raising Nuruk on its own and was able to use it. (The story of Seolhwagog comes out in Part 3.) If you use Seolhwagog, there is no taste or aroma unique to wheat Nuruk because there is no No Your Own Nuruk, No Your Own Brewery 98 Finding My Own Nuruk taste or aroma unique to wheat Nuruk. The cool fragrance such as melon or pear fragrance from non-glutinous rice flour makes K-Sool elegant. Whether my efforts were rewarded or lucky enough to win an encouragement award. A total of 76 people participated and eight winners were selected. It was a great feeling to receive an award seven years after starting K-Sool brewing. It also became an opportunity to realize Seolhwagog's potential and the importance of K-Sool balance. But at the same time I felt that there was still a long way to go.

On the day of the Changpoju Contest awards ceremony, there was a tasting event for general audiences where other winning works were tasted. Generally soft and light with acidity regardless of size or smallness were very well balanced. On the other hand, my K-Sool was bitter and poisonous, so the amount for tasting did not decrease much.

An elderly man had a drink and said, "Oh, it's poisonous." It was a really valuable time to feel with my body, not my head, how far the gap between the K-Sool I like and the K-Sool that the public would like.

Part 3

Nuruk, Nuruk, Nuruk

This is a serious Nuruk story. How can we overcome the terrible failure of last wheat Nuruk? Let's start finding our own Nuruk with burning passion.

Song Chung-seong Nuruk, in the same way as the Joseon Dynasty

Song Chung-seong, he laughed like a cow!

|

It was a phrase in the introduction of a Traditional Nuruk School instructor. 'Strong performance with a style that doesn't know how time goes by', 'Combination of practical experience and theory', 'An infant prodigof the industry'. The thought that the words expressing teacher Song Chung-seong were somewhat over-the-top disappeared within 30 minutes of the beginning of the lecture. I don't know what aspect of Nuruk made this person crazy, but from one to ten, the lecture room was filled with living stories that he had experienced directly.

Teacher Song Chung-sung, 8th Nuruk School @ Fermentation Academy Cafe Photo Capture

Open-type Nuruk Fermentation

|

Gayangju Research Institute Myungju, Myunginban Nuruk class was also excellent, but the breadth and depth of classes aimed only at Nuruk were different. First of all, the story about open-type Nuruk fermentation was very interesting. In the old days, our ancestors hung all Nuruk under the eaves. It shrank inward due to frequent alcohol bans during the Young·Jeongjo era and changed to the current sealed-type through mass production methods during the Japanese colonial period. The sealed-type method is a method of stacking layers by adjusting temperature and humidity while having a Nuruk room, as we see in Songhakgokja, Jinjugokja, and Geumjeongsanseong Nuruk.

The open-type Nuruk fermentation method is well recorded in early Joseon documents, and during class we read <Sanlimgyeongje> one sentence at a time to see what it was. Important keywords include 'It's best to start after Chobok', 'Wrap tightly with lotus leaves or dogwood leaves', 'Use yeokwe and mung bean juice', grinding rate is '10 mal of wheat per 2 mal of flour', unfortunately moisture content is not specific but 'Make dough and  step on it tightly'.(Later during practice, I added 10ml more considering the recommended amount of 220ml per 1kg of wheat and the time to go home for shaping. Compared to using 350ml or 300ml during Korea Part 3. Nuruk, Nuruk, Nuruk 103 Gayangju Research Institute practice, the amount of water is very small, but I think it's because a dedicated press molding machine was used.)

The most impressive thing in <Sanlimgyeongje> was when to start. If you start after Chobok, there is no need for separate moisture or temperature control because the environment is good enough. Indeed, as the rainy season begins around that time, Nuruk moisture evaporates slowly due to high humidity during the rainy season, and the large diurnal temperature difference suppresses excessive rise in product temperature, making it an optimal condition for mold to live. As you enter the hightemperature period of summer in earnest, mold grows towards the center with hyphae and enzyme activation is maximized to naturally lead to drying process. Quality Nuruk is produced enough to call nature itself the best Nuruk room.

I wonder if Joseon-era climate still matches modern climate and I don't believe that just hanging it up will make Nuruk. But after hearing what Lee Han-sang, CEO of Pungjeongsagye said, I felt ashamed for guessing with little knowledge.

Nuruk hanging under the eaves @[Korea liquor tour] "Four kinds of KSool from Pungjeongsagye, all tastes are different"

"I've been through trial and error for a long time, but making Nuruk is easy. If you make it only between Chobok and Jungbok on the lunar calendar or between July 10th and 20th on the solar calendar, there will be no problem. During that time when temperature and humidity are most suitable for making Nuruk, you can make it outside as well as inside. Just knead Nuruk and hang it under the eaves. That's how easy it is to make Nuruk. At other times, you can do it indoors like making cheonggukjang at home. In the past, mothers and grandmothers hung Nuruk at home and brewed K-Sool with that Nuruk. I don't understand why they say it's difficult. I make all the Nuruk I will use for a year in mid-July. This is because this time is most suitable for making Nuruk outside. However, if I make Nuruk wrong at this time, I ruin all of my year's worth of Nuruk so always be careful. It's safer to make a little bit of Nuruk several times dividedly, but I make it all at once because I can't make Nuruk outside other than that time. But I haven't failed yet. I'm confident, so I'm doing this." [41]

Mechanization, automation

After open-type Nuruk fermentation, what I learned at Nuruk School is mechanization and automation. To make Nuruk, you need whole wheat with a suitable grinding rate, and during class we used a top-opening soy milk machine.(Soy milk machines are said to be the best among various grinding methods.) There was also a Nuruk molding machine, which appeared to be self-made and initially used a jackie system, but now it is completely mechanical. There was also a dedicated Nuruk room, but since I had to tak e it home and ferment it up, I learned about a makeshift Nuruk room using a paper box.

The paper box uses a post office box and has two air holes on top that can be opened and closed with a ⊏ shaped tool. A thermometer is Part 3. Nuruk, Nuruk, Nuruk 105 inserted into the Nuruk to measure the product temperature, and a hygrometer is installed to measure the temperature and humidity of the Nuruk room. While doing so, record daily changes in the fermentation diary, imitating the aforementioned open-type Nuruk fermentation environment as much as possible.

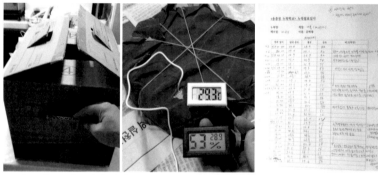

Paper box with air holes (left), thermometer for measuring Nuruk product temperature and hygrometer for Nuruk room (middle), fermentation diary (right)

For example, if the outside temperature needs to be high, wrap it or put an electric blanket underneath. If the temperature is too high, open the air hole above appropriately to lower it by evaporation heat. (Evaporation heat refers to the phenomenon of moisture taking away heat from its surroundings when it evaporates. It's the same principle as feeling cold when we come out of a bathhouse.)

Nuruk spacing can also be used to manage product temperature. At first, Nuruk was placed close together to raise the temperature and when the temperature rose enough, it was spaced apart and then very close together during

later fermentation. In practice, it was a very cumbersome and difficult task. When I asked if commercial brewing does this too, they said that everything is automated like a recent Smart Farm so there is no need for human hands. Moreover, after checking Song teacher's patent called 'Traditional Nuruk Manufacturing Device(Song Chung-sung, Registration Number:1018273780 000)', credibility increased even more.

At the time of writing this book, Song Chung-sung left Jeonnam Jangseong Cheongsanroksoo and is making a new challenge called 'Miumnet Distillery'. I wish him success in expanding his mechanization and automation range to large-scale distillers.

Making wheat Nuruk

I returned home with three pieces of wheat Nuruk made by mixing wheat and wheat bran, lotus leaves, and post office boxes. After covering it with lotus leaves and making a Nuruk house with boxes, I started fermenting it in earnest. The start date was June 13th, so the outside temperature was over 27 degrees and it was good conditions for fermentation. As I learned, I tried to control it so that the product temperature would not rise too much for 2-3 days and then tried to keep it as high as possible afterwards. On the fourth day of fermentation diary, it says 'smells savory', but this time I remember being happy that it was really going well. A week later I headed to Seochodong with Nuruk that was being ferment. It's the day of Nuruk inspection and second class.

Teacher Song checked each Nuruk one by one with its diary. The surface condition was explained why it was like that, what was inside reason why it was like that, well done part and explanation about

regrettable part continued.

The Nuruk I brought looked fine on the outside but when I split it open it was like bread on the inside. It's called lactic acid fermentation. It seemed like I knew the cause of 'savory smell'. What I thought was going well was actually making bread instead of Nuruk. It is said that this phenomenon appears due to the high amount of moisture in general. Not only me but many colleagues had lactic acid fermentation whether they had more or less. There seems to have been some mistake when making Nuruk last week. Like Mitsul, lactic acid bacteria initially dominate in Nuruk but as moisture decreases and product temperature rises mold takes its place but in this case lactic acid bacteria won. It became an opportunity to realize the importance of moisture rate and product temperature management.

Making wheat flour Nuruk

|

The second practice is wheat flour Nuruk made by pressing wheat flour. The difference from wheat Nuruk is that since it is wheat flour you pour water and mix well (don't knead) then grind with a mixer so that it doesn't stick together and then shape it.

I was very sorry for the failure of wheat Nuruk so I clenched my teeth and jumped in. 36 hours after the start of primary fermentation, 9days after entering secondary fermentation, including efforts to raise product temperature using steaming packs, and at the 14-day elapsed point, it was crushed and stored for aging. I made a report by organizing the fermentation diary and progress history with photos and sent it to teacher Song Chung-sung.

I received a reply soon, and I was relieved to hear that it was well done. One regrettable point was that the maximum fermentation temperature of wheat Nuruk was 45 degrees and wheat flour Nuruk was 38 degrees, but I mistakenly passed 40 degrees for a period of time, and due to high temperature, spores were attached inside due to cracks. The method taught by Teacher Song was very cumbersome because I had to manage the temperature and humidity of the Nuruk box several times a day, but it was easy to understand when I thought that I was hanging it like our ancestors did. In particular, the fermentation diary visualized the process and helped broaden my understanding. However, it would be nice if appropriate equipment such as a wheat grinder and a dedicated molding machine were supported, but since I am brewing a small amount in an apartment, this part still remains as a barrier.

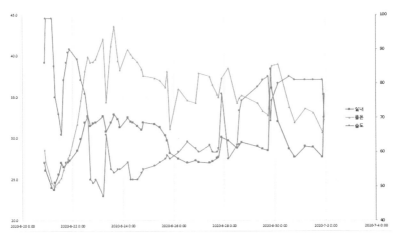

Visualization of fermentation diary data (pink is indoor temperature, gray is Nuruk product temperature, blue is humidity)

Repeated wheat Nuruk failure

|

The success of wheat flour Nuruk called for a re-challenge of wheat Nuruk. Since I don't have a separate grinder, I bought 'Nuruk-making whole wheat' on the internet. In case there is not enough fine particle amount needed for molding, I tried sifting it with a fine sieve and it looked sufficient at about 30%. With an expectant heart, I poured 220ml of water and kneaded it and tried to shape it, but contrary to expectations, it didn't stick together at all. The amount of water seemed too small. After breaking it three times, finally 430ml of water went in (moisture meter measurement 40%), but at that time I didn't know why so much water was needed. Anyway, I thought there was a lot of moisture so I made a paper box and started fermenting it up. Since there was so much moisture in it, I tried to get rid of it quickly.

I quickly removed the lotus leaf and opened many air holes, but unfortunately it overlapped with the rainy season and overall the outside temperature was around 25 degrees so the product temperature did not rise sharply. During the primary fermentation

period, I could see that Nuruk's stomach was swelling up and there was a previous 'savory smell' before.

Yes. I made bread again. It's failure.

It was clear that he failed because he had too much moisture. The problem is why molding didn't work. At that time, I thought maybe because I stepped on it with my feet but there was a dedicated molding machine at Nuruk School. Once I doubt it, everything seemed to have happened because I didn't have that machine. But there is no situation where I can bring in an expensive molding machine. While searching Google or YouTube for something else that might be an alternative, I found exactly what I wanted. It's a hydraulic press.

Super-string hydraulic commercial press

During the Nuruk School lecture, Teacher Song Chung-sung also used a jackie-type compressor that stamps bricks, and the Nuruk School molding machine also used a jackie system in the early days, so it looked like a good alternative.

Domestic compressors(juicers) were too expensive to afford, but Chinese-made ones were worth trying once. Crucially, I saw a YouTube video using the same machine to stamp(?) Nuruk and made up my mind. The principle is very simple. When you push a 3-ton jackie on a plate, there is a support above it and pressure is applied below.(See YouTube capture below)

When I finally received it after a long overseas shipment, I felt relieved that my hard work was over.

'Nuruk-making whole wheat' 1kg with 300ml of water. Nuruk School said 220ml, but referring to Myungju class, I put in 300ml. The more you knead, the more gluten comes out and it is advantageous for molding so I kneaded hard.

Now put Nuruk on a dry flour cloth and then put it in the press tank and apply pressure with a jackie… It's so disappointing that still not shaped!

I really found out what the problem was later when I asked directore Han Young-seok.(I actually took it to class!) The whole wheat I bought on the internet had almost no starch. If there is enough starch, it will absorb water and gluten will come out as you knead it, but since there was little from the beginning, it was impossible to stick. Director Han said that if you use 5% rice porridge of Nuruk amount, it sticks very well and especially the scent becomes unique due to cooked grains. Anyway, I was very angry with myself for not checking the ingredients properly and continuing to dig.

Improved Nuruk and dry yeast,
I don't want to use it again

Isn't it just alcohol?

I

   Repeated failures and frustrations in making Nuruk grew whispers within me such as 'How many people make their own Nuruk? There are many ways to reveal the personality of K-Sool, 'Isn't it just alcohol? Look at other things too.' In the meantime, I happened to come across a K-Sool brewing one-day class where I saw a recipe for distilled liquor using improved Nuruk and yeast to make Mitsul and Deossul with koji and refined enzymes. I knew it existed, but when I saw a recipe that carefully wrote down the usage and ratio, I wondered

Eumseong-gun Technology Center developed ginseng, peach Gayangju @Eumseong Autonomous Newspaper

if this would be alcohol.

While searching for the recipe needed for the experiment, I came across a report on the 'Gayangju Method Development Project using Eumseong Ginseng and Peach' conducted by Baesangmyeonjuga and Chungbuk Eumseong-gun Agricultural Technology Center in 2013. In the report, after comparing various traditional Nuruk and improved Nuruk, it was concluded that 'if you dissolve improved Nuruk in water and soak it for more than 1 hour and then put dry yeast in Nuruk water(sugok), it is most effective' and detailed the process.[11] The recipe was very simple. Wash 1kg of non-glutinous rice cleanly and steam Godubap, then activate 7%(70g) of improved Nuruk sugok and 1.6L of water(1.6 times the amount of rice) and 5%(50g) of dry yeast. When Godubap cools down, mix it to ferment. The sub-ingredient ginseng is ground and put in 7%(70g) a day later, and after 6 days, clear alcohol is Yakju and Makgeolli is drunk by Jigemi.(Peach has a reduced water volume of 1L and uses 600g instead.)

The report was very specific so it was easy to follow. On the day's record, it says 'I hear boiling sound as soon as I put it in, up to 34 degrees. It seems strong', which seems quite impressive. The alcohol was brewed in just three weeks, but very little alcohol Jigemi came out so I could feel the charm of complete fermentation.

The alcohol with ginseng smelled like ginseng, and the alcohol with peach smelled like peach, but unlike the scent, the taste was really bad because it was stale and bitter.

Just as was expected, according to the report, Yakju should be drunk with a little lemon and sugar added, but it felt even more bitter because it was no different from any other alcohol on the market that is sold by No Your Own Nuruk, No Your Own Brewery 116 Finding My Own Nuruk adding sweeteners on a large scale.

Memory of Makgeolli Kit

Another representative example where enzyme or dry yeast is used is Makgeolli Kit. If you search for Makgeolli Kit on Naver Shopping, more than 900 results are searched. Even considering errors or duplicates, it's quite a large number. Because it's easy to access and easy to differentiate with additives while not being difficult.

I was curious once in a while but not enough to spend money on it, but by chance I got a kit and decided to make it myself. The contents were also simple: powdered powder, honey, seasoning. When I opened the powdered powder, I could see some dried rice grains. It seemed like he was imitating Makgeolli in Dongdongju style. When I took a close-up photo, small pellet-shaped pieces were visible. It seems like an enzyme or dry yeast.

Powdered powder (left) close-up photo (right) pellets are visible.

Making it is really easy. Just put powdered powder in slightly lukewarm water about three times as much as usual for a few days. Compared to the ratio of rice to water in Eumseong Ginsengju and Peachju being 1:1.6, this is an enormous amount(1:3), so I wondered if this would be alcohol.

Thanks to enzymes and powerful yeasts, it boils really well. If you squeeze it while alcohol is being made for a while, carbonated alcohol like Jangsu Makgeolli will be made. After about a week or so, the alcohol ripened completely and became calm. When I tasted it, it was sourly typical old Takju taste but there was no flavor because there was too much water. Here's a big reversal. The introduction of 'seasoning'.(It actually says seasoning on the kit.)

Seasoning is nothing special, it's just white sugar.

I weighed it just in case, and it was 110g including the bag weight! Powdered powder contains 500g, so sugar accounts for a whopping 22% of the amount of rice. I felt like I knew the secret of my favorite Jangsu Makgeolli. (Jangsu Makgeolli uses aspartame or synthetic sweeteners instead of sugar, and imported rice is used, so it's not an exaggeration to say that alcohol is just mass-produced mechanically.) Even though there was so much sugar, it didn't feel very sweet. However, it was good to drink a glass at a time because it tasted like Makgeolli that I usually drink.(But somehow it feels like drinking sugar water…)

Let's go the right way
|

I think that some sweeteners or fermentation agents can be used on the path of large-scale commercial brewing or for special purposes. The sweetness that comes out as rice is saccharified will not be fundamentally different from white sugar.

If the ratio of rice to water in the above experiment was 1:0.8 instead of 1:1.6 or 1:3, the result may have been different. Nevertheless, if you can brew alcohol with Nuruk alone, there seems to be no reason to use enzymes or yeast. It is a blessing that anyone can easily make it, but there is no personality. The diverse flavors that come from the various ingredients of Nuruk and the value of my own alcohol made with Nuruk that I brewed myself are more important.

•Reference•

Calculating the amount of enzyme input

Let's take a look at the amount of enzyme input, which is an auxiliary ingredient for brewing. First, we need to know about saccharification power(sp). Saccharification power refers to the force that converts 1g of starch into glucose, and the standard saccharification power means the force required to ferment 100kg of steamed rice normally. It is known to be 2,400,000sp and when converted to 1g, it becomes 24sp. The saccharification power of various enzymes is as follows.

The saccharification power of imported enzymes is 50sp. Therefore, to saccharify 100kg of rice, 48kg is required. The saccharification power of improved Nuruk is 1,200sp.

Therefore, to saccharify 100kg of rice, 2kg is required.

The saccharification power of Cho enzyme is 3,000sp. Therefore, to saccharify 100kg of rice, 0.8kg(800g) is required. The saccharification power of refined enzymes is 30,000sp. Therefore, to saccharify 100kg of rice, 0.08kg(80g) is required.(However, if you look at the label of the Wonderful Winery refined enzyme in the picture below, it says that it is 15,000sp per 1g. Therefore, 160g is required for saccharifying 100kg of rice. Be sure to check the label.)

So how much will our traditional Nuruk's saccharification power be?

If you buy Nuruk on the market and look at the back side, it will probably say that it is usually over 300sp. If you calculate it, you need 8kg to saccharify 100kg of rice. So traditionally Nuruk usually uses 10% of the amount of rice.

Improved Nuruk (left), refined enzyme (Wonderful Winery) (middle), dried yeast (La Parisienne) (right)

Han Young-seok Nuruk, think of yourself as a microbe

Improved Nuruk, dry yeast, and the temptation of the enzyme agent were repelled and returned to my own Nuruk search path, but like a child who lost my mother's hand in the market, I couldn't move what to do.

But luckily, I met Han Young-seok, the first Nuruk master in Korea, and the director of the Han Young-seok Fermentation Research Institute at the Top Leadership Course of the Korea Gayangju Research Institute.

Director Han Young-seok giving a lecture @Suldok capture

Nuruk is microbe

|

If Song Chung-sung started his lecture on how our ancestors in the Joseon Dynasty made Nuruk, Director Han Young-seok bagan to talk about microbes. If the role of Nuruk is to provide various enzymes and yeasts through mold, Nuruk is not making it but growing mold, and eventually using that Nuruk for alcohol was the purpose. The part where he mentioned the connection between Nuruk and mold(microbes), the final product(alcohol) was fresh and my eyes brightened.(Director Han's Nuruk class was quite difficult) When I looked at everything from a microbial perspective, the front and back of the explanation fit in and it was interesting.

The key keywords are pulverization rate, moisture content, molding shape(intensity), and additionally temperature control(season), oxygen amount, raw material, wind, etc., which are closely related to each other and there are microbes in the center. It's like solving a 7th degree equation(it's too difficult) so let's think about the first 3 elements for now.(Solve a 3rd degree equation before solving a 7th degree equation…)

Microbial living environment

|

What is a good environment for microbes to live in? It is an environment with low pulverization rate, low moisture(appropriate), and weak molding intensity. The pulverization rate means how much whole wheat has been crushed. If it is 120%, it means that about 20% of flour is included.(When Part 3. Nuruk, Nuruk, Nuruk 123 1kg of whole wheat is crushed and sifted through a middle sieve, about 200g of flour comes out)

Since the pulverization rate is low, there is enough space in between and the molding intensity is weak so there will be enough oxygen. Since mold cannot live in water(a lot of moisture), it can

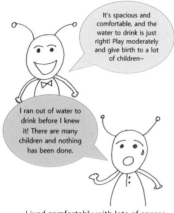

Lived comfortably with lots of spores~

reproduce comfortably if there is little moisture. The problem is that fermentation will end quickly if it is good to live in, but actually there will be less enzyme or yeast. Enzymes play a role in cutting starch into small pieces in K-Sool to saccharify it, and yeast eats that sugar to produce alcohol, so in this case it becomes alcohol with low saccharification power and low alcohol content.

Then what is an environment that is difficult for microbes to live in? If you think about it opposite to the above, it is an environment with high pulverization rate, high moisture content, and strong molding intensity. If you have a high pulverization rate and strong molding intensity, there will be no empty space inside and oxygen will be lacking due to lack of oxygen. In addition, if there is a lot of

moisture, food activity will be restricted and fermentation will take a long time and may even stop if not done well.

However, working for a long time means that there are many enzymes and yeasts, so if you brew, it becomes K-Sool with high saccharification

← A lot of hyphae in a difficult environment, and the saccharification power increased

power, stable and high alcohol content. At first glance it seems that if microbes are good to live in good(high saccharification power) Nuruk will come out but it's not interesting.

Let's take a closer look at what it means for microbes to live.

When you first make Nuruk, wrap it with raw materials such as lotus leaves, and wild molds and yeasts attached to the leaves stick to the surface of Nuruk and take root. Because mold is a living organism, it secretes enzymes while spreading its hyphae and begins to eat(cut) the starch of Nuruk, generating heat in the process. The heat generated expands the air and evaporates upwards with moisture, and oxygen is supplied in between, so the hyphae continue to spread along the moisture. The starch(glucose) and oxygen cut by the mold are good environments for yeast that proliferate in an aerobic environment, so the amount of yeast also increases. If there is a lot of moisture and it evaporates slowly, the time for cutting starch(enzyme production) and increasing yeast increases, resulting in good Nuruk with high saccharification power.

A variable called temperature control(season)

So if you create a barren environment that is difficult for microorganisms to live in, will you get good Nuruk? Let's add one more variable to the equation. The variable is temperature control(season).

First of all, in order for mold to feel like trying to live, the starting temperature must be at least 26 degrees. There will be no problem at the point where it generates heat by itself, but when the Nuruk temperature drops, it must be kept warm at least 28 degrees or higher. It may be possible to make Nuruk even in midwinter, but it is not easy. If you don't have a dedicated Nuruk room, you may not be necessary to go against nature. Even if the temperature is appropriate in summer, if there is an air conditioner nearby or directly exposed to sunlight, microorganisms feel the temperature difference and not good.

The grinding rate and amount of moisture are determined depending on which season(temperature, humidity) my Nuruk is completed. If the external humidity is high(in midsummer), the internal and external density of Nuruk becomes equal and it is difficult for internal moisture to escape outside. On the contrary, if the external humidity is low(winter), the internal moisture of Nuruk is forcibly sucked out and Nuruk splits.

Cracks occur when Nuruk receives direct sunlight and moisture suddenly pops out at once. If a crack occurs, that surface has no enzymes like Nuruk's surface and fermentation odor spreads on residual moisture and becomes bad Nuruk with soy and stale odor.

By the way, what people call Nuruk odor is different from fermentation odor due to wheat bran. Han Young-seok used wheat that has been polished to remove wheat bran odor and simultaneously extract wheat's unique scent hidden by wheat bran, there was no need to filter Mitsul and it seemed like a good idea.

Looking at the above content, Nuruk can be made from April when the outside temperature rises somewhat, and as mentioned in the previous Song chung-seong Nuruk episode, using newly harvested wheat to make before and after Chobok would be best. At this time, either put a lot of moisture with a low grinding rate or put medium moisture with a high grinding rate. If the grinding rate is low, moisture evaporates well so put a lot in it. If the grinding rate is high, evaporation will be slow so put less moisture.

In midsummer as mentioned earlier it is not good to start Nuruk with high temperature and high humidity and autumn(after Chubun) is considered good because it is called Chugok, rapid fermentation progresses with high temperature humidity at first then fermentation slows down gradually with low temperature humidity later on resulting in appropriate saccharification power and fragrance. Of course winter has a low success rate so there is no need to force floating.

You have to ride a bike yourself

It seems simple(as if I know everything), but fermentation conditions external environment etc. There are many variables so it's actually very complicated. He advised me to fix two variables among grinding rate moisture amount shaping strength only adjust one experiment while widening understanding then increase one variable at a time, it make me sympathize with. While doing so he spoke about importance of execution by comparing it with how to ride bicycle.

No matter how much you explain how not to fall to someone who can't ride a bike they can't understand but if you actually ride a bike you know without having to explain it like if you make Nuruk several times at some point you will feel it.

In two lectures master Han emphasized several times to have interest but discard haste. It means that Nuruk is finished when all the moisture in Nuruk has completely flown away and you need to be patient(never break it out in the middle) and wait until that point.

Wheat 500g with moisture content of 30% (150ml) made Gaetteog Nuruk weighed 420g so all moisture flew away and additional weight loss of about 16% occurred

For example if 1kg of wheat contains 250ml of water the water that goes in must all fly away and additionally about 20% weight loss occurs additionally during the process of changing starch (high molecular weight) to sugar (low molecular weight) due to mold feeding activity. Therefore when the final weight of Nuruk becomes 800g it is completely finished.

It is said that a post office paper box is better than styrofoam for making Nuruk and it is used completely sealed except for turning it over once every two days. The paper box itself absorbs moisture and evaporates it outside making it an excellent Nuruk room. 1kg for rice Nuruk in box No. 3 and 1kg for wheat Nuruk in box No. 2 is appropriate. Nuruk made before and after Chobok our ancestors hung it under the eaves where the wind was well shaded but it is recommened that after removing the raw material after about 3 days of inoculation when heat comes out put it in an onion net and hang it.

Gaetteog Nuruk

|

In the leader class we practiced something called 'Gaetteog Nuruk' which was different from the usual wheat Nuruk I knew so I was a little surprised at first. Then I remembered what Han said not to be attached to size. Considering the season when Nuruk is kneaded and the completion point how well can you keep microorganisms alive until the end from the perspective of microorganisms is the key.

Gaetteog Nuruk has a grinding rate of 135% with a moisture

content of 30% shaping strength is medium while the shape is small and thin at 500g. Since shaping strength is not high I can do it with just my hands using something like a bread mold. However be careful because wheat needs to be kneaded completely to absorb moisture and gluten comes out.

A slightly higher grinding rate and moisture content make it difficult for mold growth so if you make the shaping thickness thin it will dry well as autumn deepens and will be completed completely with moisture flying away in 25-30 days.

In fact I makde Gaetteog Nuruk without much difficulty and used it when brewing Yeosan Hosanchun but due to high saccharification and fermentation power was tremendous, Bansaengbansuk type Mitsul overflowing from time to time etc. One thing that was unfortunate was that due to high saccharification power and many yeasts alcohol tasted bitter but later when I asked director Han he said that this phenomenon occurred as many yeasts proliferated and died. The way to control this is not to stir Mitsul when there are many yeasts, reduce the amount of Nuruk to suppress saccharification, lower fermentation temperature etc. Anyway after squeezing out after two and a half months bitter taste decreased a lot while cold aging turned into very good K-Sool that fits my mouth with slightly bitter taste. During the lecture, director Han said that he was worried about whether high saccharification power is always the answer or whether a lot of yeast is really good. It's problem even if it's too good, I thought that Nuruk's world is very difficult.

The appearance of Gaetteok Nuruk became an opportunity to reduc burden of Tteok Nuruk. And when I looked at Nuruk as if it were microbes, even though I couldn't see them with my eyes, I could see what was happening. Just as you have to ride a bicycle yourself to learn how not to fall over, you have to make more Nuruk more often, but there are still hurdles on the material side such as buying whole wheat and proper milling.

Ryu In-soo Nuruk,
like white flowers falling on white snow

Tteog Nuruk alternative

|

Dead tired a long time with tteog Nuruk, I finally started looking for an alternative to Nuruk. (Improved Nuruk, refined enzymes, dry yeast, etc. are of course excluded) The first thing that caught my eye was heut-im Nuruk (scattered nuruk). Perhaps because I suffered too much in the Nuruk molding, if there was an alternative, I wanted to make it 'scatter' rather than 'press' if possible.

The most widely known way to make it scattered is undoubtedly koji. Koji, also known as rice Nuruk, is a method used in most breweries in our country and in Japanese sake production. It is a saccharifying agent made by inoculating specific fungi such as Aspergillus oryzae or Aspergillus kawachii into Godubap. Yeast must be added separately, but as mentioned in the previous article, the experimental results using only saccharide and yeast were really poor, so it was immediately excluded from consideration. But in the meantime, I learned an interesting fact. Our ancestors also made mold on Godubap like koji and used it.

If you look at the method of making Yeonhwa-ju written by Jeon Sunui, a court physician around 1450 in <Sanga Yorok>,

Yeonhwa Juguk @ Captured from Life and Alcohol No. 128 article

'Put mugwort on the floor and put the paper mulberry leaves on top of it, then spread out three deo of non-glutinous rice that has been steamed well and cover it with paper mulberry leaves and mugwort. After 7 days, remove the covered grass leaves and exhaust hot air for a while and put them in a bowl. After 3 days, steam one mal of non-glutinous rice until it is soft and mix it with the previously made Nuruk and put it in a jar. After 7 days, open it and use it. The amount can be estimated by this method, and lotus leaves could be laid up and down.'

According to the introduction of Heo Si-myung Makgeolli School principal, similar content is also found in <Yeokjubangmun> recorded in the mid-19th century, so this method can be seen as a technique that was communicated during the Joseon Dynasty. You may not have noticed it, but the difference between koji and Yeonhwa-ju is that it does not inoculate specific fungi but use mugwort, mulberry leaves, lotus leaves, etc. to naturally sit around mold on Godubap. This is conceptually no different from making ordinary tteok Nuruk.

A similar case can be found in modern times.

Mr. Watanabe of Rural Bakery

<Baking Capitalism at a Rural Bakery> is a story of Watanabe Itaru's

bakery startup that became a bestseller when it was published in 2014. The reason for talking about rural bakery stories out of nowhere is because Watanabe's process of having his own natural Nuruk bacteria for the yeast used in his bread is detailed in the book.

At first, Watanabe also used commercially available natural yeast like others, but he stopped using it when he realized that it was just a kind of brand different from ordinary yeast. After using natural Nuruk from nearby bean paste companies for a while, he finally decided to get his own bacteria himself. The process is interesting.

The first place he went to get bacteria was the bamboo forest behind his house. Somehow there seemed to be many good bacteria there. But Nuruk flowers bloomed quickly but failed because they were too sour to use. After that, he tried again after hearing that there were many bacteria on rice ears and failed again. He used good bacteria in Korean Makgeolli but failed again.

In the meantime, he changed the rice to organically grown organic rice and changed the board for making Nuruk from plastic to bamboo bowls through various twists and turns to realize that it is important an environment where bacteria could live. Han Young-seok director once said that if you disinfect next to Nuruk, it won't work properly. I understood this in the same context as Watanabe's case. At the end of trial and error, Watanabe finally discovered a green mold he liked inside his house. There is a scene where he realizes that the bacteria he has been looking for are inside his own house and feels empty while being happy at the same time. I feel as if it could happen to me.

And in 2021, 7 years later, in his new book <Listening to Bacteria at a Rural Bakery>, Watanabe finally makes beer with his own bacteria. From the perspective of fermentation, the use of natural Nuruk bacteria, various experiments to have one's own bacteria, and finally the process of reaching the end of fermentation, alcohol (beer), seemed to show me the way I should go.

Darumari Beer @THE JAPAN BEER TIMES, 2016 article capture

Rice heut-im Nuruk

Back to Korea and looking for heut-im Nuruk cases, Jeon Gi-bo, the representative of the brewery 'Sulbitne Jeongane' and also a senior at the Korea Gayangju Research Institute, can be found in the answer to the question of how to make and use Nuruk in the December 2020 Chosun Biz 'Park Soon-wook's K-Sool Journey' article.

"General Nuruk is a pressed Nuruk. It is made by pressing it tightly with hands or feet like Meju to form a shape and fermenting it. Pressed wheat Nuruk is the mainstream, but nowadays many breweries use rice heut-im Nuruk. The difference from wheat Nuruk is that the taste is clean and the taste deviation is small. This is actually a Nuruk made by Japanese people, but because Japan standardizes Nuruk well, sake uses this Nuruk. The problem is that our breweries use rice heut-im Nuruk called koji and all those kojis put mold into Godubap, but that mold is Japanese mold. Put Japanese mold into Nuruk to make it and use it for alcohol fermentation, and call it koji. However, our rice heutim Nuruk does not put Japanese mold into Godubap like this, but coats our unique anj-eunbaeng-i wheat flour. We may be the only one to make Nuruk like this."[11]

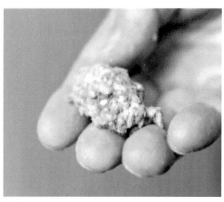

Sulbitne Jeongane heut-im Nuruk @<Agricultural Food Consumption Empathy>

In summary, it is made by sprinkling anj-eunbaeng-i wheat flour on Godubap, and various microorganisms contained in wheat flour can be seen as playing a role similar to Nuruk as they proliferate.

Representative Jeon Gi-bo also cited efficiency as a better point of scattered Nuruk than pressed Nuruk. Pressed Nuruk is too difficult to make and takes a lot of effort, and because the density is so high, the probability of going wrong is high, especially if you have to control moisture carefully. On the other hand, scattered heutim Nuruk does not have a significant drop in saccharification power and is much easier to make.

At this point, I had a strong conviction that rice heut-im Nuruk could replace wheat tteog Nuruk. However, unlike tteog Nuruk, I didn't know exactly how to make it, so I was flipping through Google or YouTube when I heard about the release of Seoul Makgeolli made by Ryu In-soo director.

Seoul Makgeolli

It was shocking in many ways.

First of all, Seoul Makgeolli put a red crown cap on a cute bottle reminiscent of a milk bottle. Wait a minute… Has there ever been a crown cap on Takju in K-Sool? In addition, a dedicated decanter is provided so that you can mix clear alcohol and Jigemi as you like, and when you pour Jigemi over clear alcohol, it visually pleases as the KSool mixes like clouds are

moving.(The fact that the name of the Makgeolli is Seoul and the label is a symbol representing Namsan, Han River, and the sun was rather cute.)

Above all, SeoulMakgeolli 'naturally' used its own Nuruk and its name is 'Seolhwagog'. The white mold that blooms on white rice flour looks like snow has fallen, so it's called Seolhwagog. The picture posted on Instagram is no different from the appearance of snow piled up in small piles.

Snowfall on Nuruk @Seoul Brewery Instagram capture

By the way, is Seolhwagog heut-im Nuruk?

Seolhwagog

|

Seolhwagog is Non-glutinous rice heut-im Nuruk. And I've already learned twice how to make it? How this is possible is that Korea Gayangju Research Institute K-Sool course is, as mentioned before, a 3-month course of Myungju, Myungin, and Juin. If you learn wheat Nuruk in Myungju class, Myungin class teaches you how to make rice Nuruk Ihwagog and Seolhwagog. I started the K-Sool course in December 2016 and although I only did Myungju·Myungin class, it was something I learned once at that time.(Strictly speaking, the fact that I attended that class was an old Naver band video with familiar faces!)

The second time was, to enter the Korea Gayangju Research Institute leadership course, a diploma from the K-Sool course is required, but rather than just listening to the last Juin course, I decided to listen to the entire course again, so I learned it again while completing it once more in January 2021. This time I vowed never to forget it again and filmed all the courses on video and carefully wrote down every word of Director Ryu's words.(The entire method of making it including my experimental results is included in Part 4 so please refer to it.)

I saw Seoul Takju and knew how to make it but I had doubts if this would make alcohol. The process was too too too simple. The only way to dispel doubts is to try it yourself. (Hands precede head!)

Repeated failures

|

Even Seolhwagog, which I thought was easy, failed twice in a row and I was devastated.

The first failure stemmed from a minor mistake.

Now there is a rice milling machine (Dolora) at home but I always went down to the local mill to get rice flour. Maybe my mind was in a hurry and I put it in without sifting through the rice flour. Did he really think that if he put rice flour in and left it for a few days, he would have a decent Nuruk as Director said? The result was a big failure. Have you ever smelled a sewer? Green spots appeared here and there and smelled bad. The temperature rose but it was like growing rotten mold. When I missed or made mistakes in simple things that I thought I knew at the execution stage, I realized once again that basics are important.

오후 2:35

류인수 소장
너무 질게 된 부분이 있는것같아요 ^^ 수분을
충분히 빼고 채로쳐서 다시 한번 해보시죠~

오후 2:37

Immediately challenged again with determination. This time I used enough moisture to dry out and sifted well through an intermediate sieve so that there were no lumps. And like the wheat Nuruk I learned before, I opened it more than once a day and wiped it up and down if there was moisture on it. But this time it failed again.

How disappointed he was that day his blog was full of regrets.

"The temperature starts to rise...

A faint yellow color with a weak sewer smell...

The aura of failure is felt.

A fundamental improvement plan seems necessary

It doesn't seem like Nuruk will just happen if left alone..."

In order to find the cause of failure, I recorded everything I did from start to finish. As I reviewed, one by one, things that could be problematic appeared.

First of all, the surrounding temperature. In the 2016 lecture, it was said that it would rise well between 20 and 25 degrees, but in the 2021 lecture, it had to be set at 24-25 degrees and insulation was needed if it was low. Looking at the fact that Han Young-seok said during the top leadership lecture that the minimum temperature for Nuruk to rise is 26 degrees, it is certain that a certain external temperature is required for Nuruk to become. Since the first attempt at Seolhwagog was on March 13th, the outside temperature would not have been high enough. One thing is for sure. The initial temperature for raising Nuruk will be over 25 degrees.(26 degrees for stability)

Next is the use of seed Nuruk. The Korea Gayangju Research Institute that there are always microorganisms necessary for alcohol because the whole world is alcohol and Nuruk, but I thought that I might not be the case.(To put it simply, the terroir is barren.) In the case of tteog Nuruk, it usually lays or covers the surroundings with grass and wraps Nuruk with lotus leaves to induce bacteria, but heut-im Nuruk cannot do that. Therefore, even a little bit of Nuruk that becomes a seed must be put in. Director Ryu's words came to mind that I should put in 1% of total amount of rice in a fine powder form.

Finally succeeded(Seolhwagog #1)

|

According to the record at the time, about 32 hours after starting, it was 'the smell is right between Nuruk and spoilage'. In other words, a suitable temperature and seed Nuruk barely crossed the ridge of decay and entered the fermentation area. Although it was not visible to the eye, I could feel the movement of microbes on my skin.

How happy I was after passing one ridge, at the end of an email sent to Ryu In-soo,

"Director Ryu In-soo,

In fact, except for those made and succeeded at research institutes or academies in the case of wheat Nuruk, I have never personally succeeded by myself. But this time Seolhwagog is still not sure whether it will succeed or not, but it is progressing without being ruined on the third try, so I don't know how good it is.

I hope it goes well until the final K-Sool comes out and I know you are busy but I would appreciate it if you could also take an interest and watch.

Kim Hyuk-rae"

National Gayangju Brewer Selection Competition, 2020

It is the largest K-Sool contest in Korea, both in name and reality. I saw an article that the number of participating teams in 2021 was 207 teams, so you can guess the scale. In addition, it is unique in that it analyzes alcohol content, sugar content, and acidity to give me a more objective understanding of the position of my K-Sool, although only for works that have advanced to the finals.

I have participated every year since 2019, but the first year I couldn't even submit, the second year I advanced to the finals but failed to win a prize, the third year I won a commendation award, and last year (2022) I failed to advance to the finals. Regardless of whether or not I won a prize, I would like to summarize what I learned through analyzing the entries for the Brewer Selection Competition.

김혁래 多精 (HyuckRae Kim)

Made by minimizing the amount of Nuruk to 4% of the amount of rice and adding various flavors using dry hopping techniques.

Alcohol(%): 17.4   Sugar content(Br): 15.1   Acidity(%): 0.321

In 2020, when I advanced to the finals, I received a leaflet about my entry work, which included analysis results along with each K-Sool introduction.(See my introduction above.)

In 2020, it was conducted in two parts: Soongok Yakju and Gahyang Yakju, and a total of 176 teams applied and 15 K-Sools received awards.(I challenged Gahyang Yakju.) Looking at the ingredients of Gahyang Yakju who came to the finals, there are pine needles, lotus leaves, pine shoots, yellow sapwood trees, rugosa rose/fruits, native tangerine peel (dried tangerine peel), roses, omija, Gapyeong pine nuts, tangerines, apples, etc., and it was noticeable that Hyangon-guk and Yeonhwa-jugog were used. Various fragrances were used, but only hops, magnolia flowers, tangerine peel (tangerine peel), and pine scent (pine needles/pine shoots) were actually selected for entry. It seemed that lotus leaves or fruit species had little impact. (I thought lotus leaves are too common and fruits may not have as much fragrance as expected.)

The fact that hops were used twice showed that the fragrance effect was great and that the citrusness of tangerines or the grass and wood or forest scent that can be felt from pines also showed that they go well with KSool.(Note that hops can only be added in fruit form and cannot be used legally in pellet form.) The sugar content of the awarded K-Sools ranged from 18.55 Brix to 27.51 Brix. Since my sugar content is 15.1 Brix, it can be seen that the awarded is quite sweet and it can be inferred that it must be sweetened to increase the likelihood of winning a prize. When Soongok Yakju's winning K-Sool analysis, there was a lot of Samyangju and it was re-etched point that good K-Sool comes out in proportion to the hard work.

The following year in 2021 is when I won a commendation award using Seolhwagog. Like Changpoju Contest, Seolhwagog played a part.

Referring to last year's analysis results, it was good to make it with Samyangju but I don't know why it came out so dry. This is my alcohol description introduced in the leaflet.

"Use self-made Nuruk in heut-im Nuruk form and manufacture according to Samyangju method. Alcohol (%): 17.2 Sugar(Bri): 11.8 Acidity(%): 0.31"

Looking at my blog at the time when I bottled my entry K-Sool, I definitely adjusted it to 18.5 Brix but whether fermentation happened more in between or whether I measured it wrong... It's still unknown.(Would I have won a bronze medal if I had been sweeter?)

Anyway, after analyzing last year's winning K-Sools again this year. Of the total of 14 K-Sools that won awards, four explicitly stated Seogtanju, means that sweet and soft alcohols performed well as expected.(Seogtanju is a representative sweet and soft K-Sool with Mitsul made with porridge and a rice:water ratio of 1:0.8.) What was unusual was alcohol content, most Takju winning works had an alcohol content below 16 degrees Celsius; especially gold medal works had an acidity of 0.62 at 11.8 degrees with 23.3 Brix; in other words, very light, sweet and sour alcohol. As I felt in the Changpoju Contest, light alcohol seems to be the trend rather than strong and bitter alcohol. And it seems that a strong acidity is added here.

My K-Sool, which has the second lowest sugar content(11.8 Brix) and the lowest acidity(0.31%), is thought to have won a prize solely due to the Seolhwagog effect, and through this contest, I have added the question of whether to make K-Sool that suits my taste or to make that suits the taste of the judges.

Part 4

My Own Nuruk

At the end of a long journey, Seolhwagog, whom I met, was
definitely the Nuruk I was looking for, but I couldn't call it my own
Nuruk. This is because only those made with microbes grown
entirely in my home environment(terroir) can be called my own
Nuruk. And I don't know how to use them well. Let's try a little
harder until my Nuruk leads to my own K-Sool.

Completely mine,
various experiments

Once the recipe was confirmed, I wanted to make Seolhwagog completely mine. To do this, various experiments were needed and roughly the following questions were the basis.

What kind of sieve is good when sieving rice flour? Medium sieve? Fine sieve? What happens if you don't use seed Nuruk? If you use it, what's good? Is it good to put wheat flour? If so, how much should I put in? Does using sub-ingredients(juice) really have an effect? What subingredients are good to use? How much sub-ingredients should I put in? What kind of rice is good to use? Glutinous rice? Brown rice? Black rice? Will using organic rice bring better results? Is it possible with mixed grains? What happens if you extend the fermentation period? What happens if you keep it? What happens if you increase the molding strength?

How big should the Nuruk mold(siru) be? Can I use something huge?

I solved the easiest problem first.

Nuruk mold (siru)

|

Seolhwagog uses a stan siru as a Nuruk mold. The bottom of the Nuruk mold is flat so that it adheres to the floor and the inside siru plate is slightly floating, which is advantageous for draining moisture below. The lid also has a pointed center like a pyramid, so even if moisture condenses, it does

not fall directly but flows down the wall side by side, preventing rice flour from rotting.

The stan siru used for K-Sool brewing is mostly made by Daechang Stainless Steel and comes in two versions: high and low. Each is divided into 40 and 28 sizes, for a total of four types. Since I bought the smallest 28 square siru(2.4kg) with low height at first to test it alone at home, I needed a larger siru because the amount of rice that can be done at once was less than 2kg.

The remaining three types of siru are two 4kg and one 8Kg. If I had my way, I would have wanted to buy the largest size, but just in case I asked

40 size square siru(8kg)
395(D)×395(W)×155(H)

40 size square siru(4kg)
395(D)×395(W)×100(H)

director Ryu which one would be good to buy, he said, "Even if you use an 8kg one, the actual amount is about 5kg and you can't increase it indiscriminately because it doesn't work well due to excessive heat rise etc. Wouldn't it be better to find the best way at your current size?" It is an opinion that seemed reasonable and I purchased an additional 40 square siru(4kg) with low height.

Seed Nuruk

Next is about seed Nuruk. At first, I used about 1% fine Nuruk by sieving Geumjeongsanseong Nuruk, but since it seemed better to use the same rice Nuruk(Ihwagog) series, I have been using Baegumdo Rice Nuruk ever since. Whether using wheat Nuruk or rice Nuruk, there was no problem at first, but after a long winter and no Ihwagog available for immediate use, I used Han Youngseok wheat Nuruk and ran into a big problem.

Seolhwagog didn't have any seolhwa (white mold) on it! Instead, yellow fungus appeared on the surface like Huanggu mushroom and turned almost green while turning yellow enough to be noticeable.

When sieved, it smelled strongly like typical wheat Nuruk and even alcohol brewed with this Seolhwagog had strange characteristics such as color or taste or fragrance similar to using wheat Nuruk. Now that I think about it, it's a natural result but just in case I used that Nuruk as seed Nuruk and brewed next Nuruk but inherited all of its previous properties.

After spending one winter season, there may have been changes in our home environment(terroir), and Han Young-seok wheat Nuruk may have influenced differently from Geumjeongsanseong Nuruk, but one thing for sure is that a precise and proper starter, that is, seed Nuruk is definitely necessary.(Fortunately, after changing to Baegumdo Rice Nuruk, Seolhwa reappeared.)

I also experimented with what would happen if I didn't use seed Nuruk at all. In this case, it was actually difficult to predict which mold would grow. It seemed like the surrounding microbes were attached at that point and the Nuruk substrate made just before seemed to have an influence.

And overall, the speed at which Seolhwagog was raised was slow. This means that it took time for the initial microbes to settle in, reminding us that seed Nuruk management is essential until the environment is fully controlled(for example, until I have my own Nuruk room). But what if you use white-koji mold or beer yeast as seed Nuruk?

White-koji mold

I happened to have white-koji mold from Suwon Fermentation Research Institute that I had bought for experimentation before. I only used a very small amount, but yellow mold appeared on the surface and it didn't turn green/bronze like wheat Nuruk but remained yellow until the end. The surface became rough but there was little feeling of mold growth and instead the product temperature remained very high for a very long time.

I sieved it after letting it cool enough, and overall it became much harder and even the inside turned yellow and some looked slightly purple. The scent was generally sour and gave a unique impression different from the existing one.

It was a while before I brewed K-Sool with Seolhwagog using white-koji mold, but for some reason Seolhwagog had a very dark brown color almost like chocolate. It was dried on May 15 last year and put in, and the date Jumo started was January 23 of the following year, so it's been almost half a year. Something seems to have happened in between, but I can only guess that fermentation continued little by little.

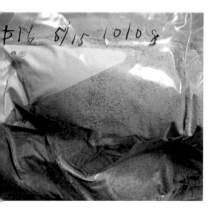

When making Jumo, unlike others, spores did not float and there were no molds on top of Seolhwagog, which seemed to be related. And one thing worth noting is that the saccharification power seemed to be much stronger than others. When stirred with a ladle, it was easier to stir at an earlier stage. Of course, this characteristic seems to have come from white mold. Is it because the fungus is very strong and survived well? Because it continued fermentation for a long time, more enzymes would have been produced.

Although the color of alcohol is dark brown and regrettable, the taste is sweetly deep while being supported by acidity and has good balance. In particular, compared to any previous Seolhwa Oyangju experiment, it felt more deep and saccharification seemed to have taken place more. There is no aversion to using specific fungi, but there is no need to damage the color of alcohol. Until the cause of Nuruk color change is revealed, unfortunately here is the end.

French Sejong Ale Yeast

As more young brewers emerge, new attempts are also increasing. A representative example is the attempt to separate saccharification and fermentation(called independent two-step fermentation) like beer, and the attempt to create a unique flavor with a distinctive beer yeast. The former case is Mark Holy Makgeolli made by Amazing Brewing Company, a well-known brewery in Seongsu-dong. It may be possible for a beer company

to make Korea traditional liquor, but they have applied their beer production know-how to K-Sool, matching the process with refined enzymes for saccharification and beer yeast for fermentation, and also brought out long-awited telecommunication sales.(Currently, Korea traditional liquor is the only alcohol that can be purchased on the Internet.) Amazing Brewing representative Kim Tae-kyung said that he chose French Sejong Ale after 24 different yeast experiments.

The attempt to enhance the flavor of K-Sool using French Sejong Ale yeast can also be found at DOK Brewery's Gyangjeulgyeo Makgeolli.

Let's hear from DOK CEO Lee Kyu-min.

"We added imported yeast to our native Makgeolli, Gyangjeulgyeo, with reverse thinking. Gyangjeulgyeo used Nuruk, but in addition, we used some French Sejong (Belgian yeast with a strong fruit scent) beer yeast. One of the reasons for using Sejong yeast is because it gives a slightly sour feeling(a kind of scent that comes from cheonggukjang and Nuruk), and a slightly rough scent. It feels a bit like natural wine. Rather than being clean, it has a slightly rough feeling, similar to Nuruk. When making Mitsul for the first time, we put Sejong yeast together with traditional wheat Nuruk."

The editorial was a bit long, but using beer yeast with Nuruk was a very unique experience. First of all, Sejong yeast was small particles of brown color and had a peculiar soybean paste smell. I seemed to know why DOK CEO said 'a slightly sour feeling' earlier. The heat rose and showed a vigorous appearance that was completely covered in a short time. When I sieved it, the brown-colored yeast disappeared and I couldn't see any at all, and the soybean paste smell completely disappeared and it was amazing.

I tried brewing K-Sool using beer yeast with high expectations for Seolhwagog, but the result was not extraordinary. The scent was not bad at Mitsul stage but the color was dark brown and not good to look at. When stirring with a ladle, compared to alcohol using rice Nuruk as a comparison target, I could definitely feel more resistance and knew that alcohol was less ripe. In addition, as Deos-sul continued, black particles continued to float on the surface of alcohol, which I thought might be due to excessive mold spores. Ultimately, alcohol was made with a sweet and sour taste of dark color, but it did not meet expectations and I don't think I will use beer yeast in the future.

Flour
|

The question of whether flour should be added when making Seolhwagog can be found in Director Ryu In-soo's opinion on flour. Director Ryu mentioned Ssias-sul, flour, Nuruk law as a way of brewing without failure and said that 30% of flour should be added compared to Nuruk amount. Some materials say that even if you brew without flour or use Nuruk made with flour, you can brew without adding it, but it seems better to use flour for safe fermentation, slight acidity and quick sedimentation induction.(Later I found out that Seolhwagog used in SeoulMakgeolli does not contain flour.)

Intermediate sieve or fine sieve
|

The size of sieve used when sieving rice flour is not a big topic I have thought about. In class we used an intermediate sieve but when looking at other materials there were some that said to use fine sieve. If rice flour particles become larger internal spores can be created and mold scent can occur due to this so it seems like a valid argument.

Or rather than particle size can be seen as grinding degree and as mentioned earlier in Han Youngseok Nuruk class if grinding degree is high microorganisms have difficulty living so high saccharification power Nuruk is made so there seems to be some consistency.

Sub-ingredients (juice)

|

The reason why rice Nuruk is put close to 30% compared to rice amount when brewing Samyangju or higher is because saccharification and fermentation power are insufficient. In the case of fermentation, yeast can be grown through multiple infusions to increase strength, but saccharification power is dependent on the amount of enzymes originally created so it is not easy. The best way to overcome this problem is to use special sub-ingredients(juice) when making Nuruk.

The initial state with white snow (left), the state where the fungus continues to grow and turn black (middle), and the state completely covered with black (right)

Yeonnip, melon, ginger, and radish are representative juice-usable ingredients, and in my case I used melon in spring and summer and radish in autumn. The application method is simple. After sprinkling the juice made in advance with a juicer on the rice flour ground finely with a dolrora, sieve it. I used about 100ml based on 4kg of rice, but if you think the moisture content of soaked rice flour is high, you need to leave it out for a little longer so that the total moisture content does not become too high. Especially in the case of radish juice, since the moisture content of radish is as high as 95.3%, it would be better to use radish juice from the moment when rice is soaked in water. By the way, there is a patent [14] for 'the method of brewing starch raw materials using saccharification enzymes of radish juice', which adds credibility to the use of juice when making Nuruk.

In fact, I experimented to see if there was a difference in brewing between using radish juice and not using it. In Oyangju brewing conducted with the same recipe only with different Seolhwagog, when stirring at Mitsul stage, the side without juice had more resistance and could tell that saccharification power was low and progress was slower. Even when Chaeju was finally done and alcohol was made, in the case where juice was not added, there were more floating rice grains and Jigemi than the comparison target so it was confirmed that fermentation power also decreased along with saccharification. In other words, it is essential to use sub-ingredients(juice) when making Seolhwagog.

Molding strength

|

After evenly spreading the rice flour for Seolhwagog in a sieve, hit it on the floor 2-3 times and lift it up. But what if you press down on the inside with your palm or a heavy object to make it tight? According to Director Han Young-seok's words, if grinding degree is high and molding strength is high, mold will have difficulty living so it takes longer and instead saccharification power increases

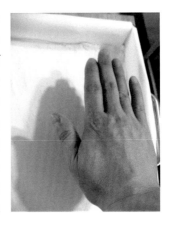

but I wanted to see if this was really true. I didn't use any special tools but increased strength by pressing down on rice flour with my fingers and palms.

However, it didn't seem like fermentation time took longer than usual and even brewing results using that Nuruk were not much different so I couldn't find any difference. If I try again I would like to press down with something heavier and stronger than my palm but for this part I will have to wait until next time.

Fermentation period

|

It is time to talk about the most important item among various conditions and methods of experiment using Seolhwagog. It is the fermentation period. When I was learning Seolhwagog, I was told to stop fermentation and sift it to dry it if I saw white mold on the surface, but I vaguely thought that it would be better if I left it a little longer. It was because Director Han Young-seok's words, "The amount of enzymes and yeast increases because mold moves along with damp and continues to multiply while wet" came to mind.

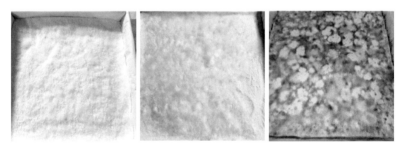

The initial state with white snow (left), the state where the fungus continues to grow and turn black (middle), and the state completely covered with black (right)

In addition, sifting as soon as white mold was seen resulted in continued post-fermentation during the drying process. Even if you turn it over often, the rice flour that is clumped together is hot and the molds continue to work. This phenomenon, along with the words of Director Han Youngseok, fueled the idea that it could be left a little longer.

Once I decided to wait and see, Seolhwagog was covered in white mold in a short time. As the core temperature was high, the white mold turned black again and became richer(?) and thicker.

I was worried about how to get through the thick fungus forest, but there was nothing too difficult. Gently scrape the mold off the surface with a spoon and it comes off easily. I happened to see Geumjeongsanseong Nuruk-related programs grinding surface mold with a grinder, and I thought that all Nuruk do that.

Rather than surface fungus, the side of the steamer was the problem. As the fermentation continued, the side that came in contact with the steamer was exposed to moisture for a long time and became hard like rubber. I cut and used this part as if I were cutting bread, and it was fun as if I was cutting a large loaf of bread made in siru. The hyphae spread to the inside of the Nuruk, so it became hard like Baekseolgi Rice Cake rather than castella, so I used a large kitchen knife to actually cut it.

Cutting the hard part(left),sifting (middle), remaining hard part after sieving (right)

Thanks to the long fermentation period, the drying time was shortened.

I thought I had a higher quality Nuruk with more saccharification power. Now, I believed that this would create my own cool K-Sool, but while brewing, I had an ominous feeling that I was going in the wrong direction. First of all, the color of the drink was strange. From Jumo, it was very dark and close to brown in severe cases. The more Deos-sul was repeated, the lighter it became, but the color of the finished drink was brown, so I didn't feel like drinking it. In addition, there were many black grains floating in the drink. Now that I think about it, it seems to be mold spores, and it hasn't completely disappeared no matter how many times I scoop it up, but I lost interest at the thought of drinking moldy K-Sool. It is difficult for spores to enter the Tteog Nuruk, which is made with a firm step, but in the case of Heut-im Nuruk, which is loose, there is a lot of space inside, so not only enzymes but also spores can spread widely, so it seems to be more so.

Suddenly, the words of a certain article by Director Han Yeong-seok came to mind.

'Nuruk moldy on the outside of fermenting Nuruk is not a good thing. If humidity control fails, mold blooms a lot, CEO Han Young-seok said.

"If there are many mold spores on the surface of Nuruk, the outer surface is coated with mold." "In this case, the humidity inside the Nuruk cannot escape, and mold cannot penetrate inside, so highquality

Nuruk cannot be made," he said. No matter where I looked around the Nuruk room at Han Young-seok's Fermentation Research Center, I couldn't find a Nuruk with a lot of fungal flowers.' "

After listening to Director Han Young-seok's words, it seemed that it was not necessary to keep it for a long time just to recklessly increase the saccharification power. Humidity control was said to be the key, but there was a limit to sophistication, such as leaving the steamer lid open at an angle or placing a bowl on the bottom. However, sifting right away as soon as you see mold doesn't seem to be the answer... Every time I run into a problem, the only person who ultimately believes is Director Ryu In-soo, so I asked a question about this once or twice, and the contents of what he said are as follows.

"If you see mold on the surface, you should stop. Seolhwagog does not use mold, it uses enzymes. Instead, it is important to remove enough moisture. That way, the fragrance becomes stronger." "In the case of the research institute, if you see white mold, leave it for another 5 hours, cover the top with a cloth and support the bottom with a tree, etc., and leave it for 12 hours. After sifting, focus on drying

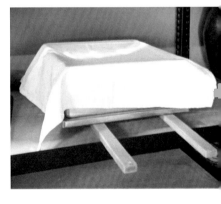

completely. If possible, blow air with a fan and keep making furrows with a rake. Of course, yeast and enzymes are not enough, so I use 30%."

I can't remember where I read it, but it is said that koji for making sake is slowly dried. It is said that it is because the koji is dried and the flavor component is strengthened, but it seems to be in the same context as the director said.

There is one tip when drying Seolhwagog. At first, I spread vinyl on a flat plate like the Korea Gayangju Research Institute and sprayed Nuruk to dry it, but later the vinyl changed to paper, so I asked. It is said that vinyl does not release moisture during drying, so if done wrong, Nuruk may be ruined by post-fermentation. When I dried the paper on the actual paper, I found that the paper absorbs the remaining moisture and blows it away, reducing the drying time and improving the final result. (Don't throw away the used paper, but put it down later. It's better as if you put thicker paper on it, so don't throw it away and save it.)

Did they say that the end of tuning is a genuine product?

I turned around and finally came to the first way.

My Home Seolhwagog,
How to Make My Own Nuruk

Based on the experiments so far, I will summarize how to make my own Nuruk in Seolhwagog at home.

1. Preparation (Based on 2kg of rice flour)

· Prepare 2kg of Non-glutinous rice flor.

- If frozen, thaw sufficeintrly.

- It prevents the rice flor from absorbing too much moisture.

  (Drain enough water)

· Prepare Daechangsten squre streamer No. 28(2.4kg) with Nuruk mold.

- For 4kg of rice flour, use square streamer No.40(4kg)

· Nuruk house is made by folding paper and inserted into a streamer.

- See below how to make a Nuruk house

After cutting the paper into squares, put the siru board on it and fold it in four directions. After removing the siru board, fold the three corners in one direction and insert it into the siru, cut the upper part with scissors and fold it back to complete the Nuruk house.

- See below how to make a Nuruk house
  · Prepare seed Nuruk within 2% of the amount of rice.
- In my case, I use Baegeum Rice Nuruk 40g
· Prepare flour within 2% of the amount of rice.
- Im my case, I use 40g of soft flour
· Prepare about 50ml of melon or radish juice as a secondary ingredient.
- If the amount of rice flur moisture is too much, reduce the amount.
- In case of melon, it can be used with the skin on.

2. Fermentation

· After mixing the ingredients, sift them through a fine sieve and put them into the Nuruk mold.
- Mix rice flour, seed Nuruk, wheat flour and secondary ingredients.
- When adding the juice of the secondary ingredients, sprinkle evenly little by little to prevent clumping.
- After thoroughly mixing, mix well and sift through a fine sieve.(It is good to collect the ingredients left in the sieve and use them when making other K-Sools.)

- Put the sifted flour into a Nuruk mold, level it on top, and hit it on the floor several times to compack it.
· Monitor progress.
- If the outside temperature is low, cover whith clothes to keep warm.
- Touch it occasionally to see if it feels warm.
- When the core temperature rises, open it once and wipe the streamer lid and moisture from the bottom.
- At this time, check for white mold on the surface.
- If white mold is not visible, repeat the above process.
· If you see white mold, start cooling.
- Open the lid of the streamer, and make a space by placing a tree or bowl underneath.
- Cover the top of the streamer with a cotton cloth and cool slowly for about 12 hours.
- After 12 hours, go to the drying stage.
· If there is a lot of humidity and white mold or black mold blooms, go directly to the drying stage.

3. Drying
· Prepare a drying rack by laying paper on a large tray.
- Paper is used to facilitate the release of moisture during drying.
- When the drying rack is ready, sift though an intermediate sieve.
- If you see mold on the surface or sides, scrape it off.
- It is easier to turn the whole streamer over and take it out than scooping out Seolhwagog bit by bit.

- Cut Seolhwagog and sieve it.
· Divide the sifted Seolhwagog into appropriate amounts and place them on a drying rack.
- It is easy to dry when spread out as thinly as possible.
- Occasionally use your hand or a rake to loosen clumps and turen them over or valley them.
- Be careful not to cause post-fermentation during drying
· Dry enough to fly Seolhwagog powder.
- It usually takes about 3 days to dry completely.

- If you put it in a state that is not sufficiently dried, be careful as pos-fermentation will occur in that state.
- Weigh the dried Seolhwagog, subdivide it according to the amount you normally use, and put it in a zipper bag.

4. Save

· Prepare a storage room in a dry place away from sunlight.
- Store distributed bags of Seolhwagog in the storage room.
- It is good to put a dehumidifier together to remove any moisture.

Brewing K-Sool with Seolhwagog

First Try

I

After twists and turns, Seolhwagog was created, but I was still not sure if it would become a drink. I decided to use Samyangju because the amount of yeast was small, and I envisioned a recipe with 25% Seolhwagog at a ratio of 1:1 to rice.

	Rice	Water	Nuruk	Method
Mitsul	0.5	1.5	1.5(Seolhwagog)	Beombeog
Deos-sul1	1	3		Beombeog
Deos-sul2	3			Glutinous rice Godubap
	4.5	4.5	Total amount 9L	
	1	: 1	Nuruk 25%	

I ran into difficulties from the start. In the case of ordinary wheat Nuruk, 4~5% of the total amount of rice is used when using Ssias-sul, so if there was no problem when mixing with Mitsul, 25% of Seolhwagog was used, so it was very difficult to mix with Beombeog.(It is equivalent to pouring 1.5L of water into 2kg of rice flour, so the

amount of water is only 75% of the amount of rice.) In addition, the speed at which alcohol boils was different from what we usually see, so it was difficult to match the timing of Deos-sul. It started to boil after about 5 days, including the 1st Deos-sul, but even that was not as good as expected, so I struggled.

Anyway, Glutinous rice was already washed, and out of impatience that the alcohol wouldn't work, I decided to add 3.6g of purified enzyme, half the amount of rice.(Refer to 'Calculating the amount of enzyme input' for the method of calculating the input amount of purified enzyme)

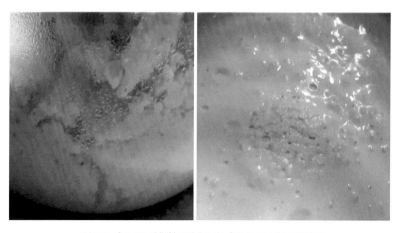

12 hours after Mitsul (left), 3rd day, the first Deos-sul proceeding despite lack of preparation (right)

I took Chaeju after almost two months of drinking.

It smelled pretty strong, and Jigemi looked like yoghurt.(Actually, it smelled like dairy products.) As for the taste of alcohol, the sour taste was felt first, followed by the sweet taste, and the bitter alcohol adorned the end. While I was thrilled that this amount of alcohol could be produced with just Seolhwagog, I felt regret that I should not have added enzymes.

Incredible melon scent, pear scent

|

Now that I've confirmed that Seolhwagog alone can make alcohol, I wanted to find a recipe that was just right for me. I checked the Mitsul change several times a day to find the point of Deos-sul that was the most problematic. Beombeog, which looked hard, was released to some extent, but it took about 2 to 3 days, and after 4 days, it started to boil and continued for a long time.

Let's look at the blog I wrote on the 4th day at the time.

"Wednesday, 5/19
It's still boiling on the 4th day, so I can't do Deos-sul. I was going to do it if possible, but when I put my nose to it, it was full of carbon dioxide."

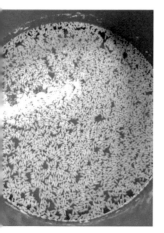 In the end, the 1st Deos-sul took place over 5 days, and the 2nd Deos-sul also took place after 4 days. This process helped a lot in understanding the characteristics of Seolhwagog I made. This time, I did Chaeju in a month and a half to avoid the heat. The grains of rice floated beautifully, and above all, the fragrance was amazing. Whether it was a melon or a pear, it had a sweet yet cool scent. It was the second liquor I made with my Seolhwagog following the last one, but I was delighted that it was made with only rice, water, and my Nuruk without any additives.

Won a prize at the Gayangju Brewer Selection Competition

I decided to apply for the Gayangju Brewer Selection Competition ('21), which I had suffered several times. The problem is that Asan Clear Rice Samkwang Non-glutinous rice sent by the organizers must be used. The same amount or at least 70% of water must be used for the last Deos-sul to decompose the non-glutinous rice, so the quantity increased somewhat.

	Rice	Water	Nuruk	Method
Mitsul	0.5	1.7	1.28(Seolhwagog)	Beombeog
Deos-sul1	1	1.5		Beombeog
Deos-sul2	4	3.25		Non-glutinous rice Godubap
	5.5	6.45	Total amount 11.95L	
	1	1 : 1.17	Nuruk 23%	

As before, after spending 5 days on Mitsul and 4 days on Deos-sul 1, I mixed it with Godubap, a non-glutinous rice fermented in hot water the day before, and had Chaeju in less than a month due to the competition schedule. After aging for one week, it was filtered under reduced pressure and submitted. Chaeju It was difficult to squeeze because the point of view was fast, but everything was enjoyable because the fragrance was good.

The feeling is embedded in the blog at the time.

"9/21 Chaeju

The first impression is that it fermented more than I thought, and the yellow color is good. It smells like melon. Jigemi is difficult to squeeze, and the remainder looks thick like milk. The amount of alcohol seems to be quite high. When I tasted it, milky, spicy, melon, pear, pretty sweet(very cool taste, scent)"

As I mentioned in the K-Sool competition entry, I finally won a prize in a major K-Sool competition with the third K-Sool I made with my Seolhwagog.

The door that would not open even after knocking on it was finally open. I believe it was because I used my Nuruk entirely. And I'm sure it's because the Nuruk isn't normal.(It is not ordinary because my Nuruk is a product that reflects my environment(terroir).

My own Nuruk, which was born with my own terroir that exists nowhere else in the world, gave a revolutionary meaning to K-Sool brewing, which had been competing with Nuruk purchased from someone else's recipe.

And I instilled strong pride and vitality in being different from others.

Now, a new turning point has come.

Which K-Sool recipe is perfect for my Nuruk?

Seolhwagog became a new turning point in K-Sool making, but it also brought a lot of homework. First of all, I need a lot of rice flour. There was a mill that I knew well in the neighborhood, but it was not easy to carry out the rice flour soaked in moisture every time on time. Besides, getting the Deos-sul perspective was still a problem. Based on Samyangju, I put it on the 5th and 4th, but I wasn't sure if that was correct.

Continuously making K-Sool without rice flour

The rice flour problem got an idea from 'If you want to get a continuous drink' in the brewing method of <Eumsik Dimibang>. It is the so-called one-year K-Sool. Based on 10L of K-Sool over Samyangju, 7L of Chaeju is stirred well, and rice, water, and 7L of Nuruk are added to the remaining 3L to continuously make K-Sool.

In this way, it is possible to maintain a similar taste of alcohol and simplify the process, but it is attractive because there is no need to make rice flour decisively. However, Nuruk needs to be sufficiently activated with Ssiassul, fine Nuruk, or sugok, but Seolhwagog has a large amount, so I thought it would cover that much. Crucially, I was relieved to see that teacher Ki-myung Kim, who took the leadership class together, was using the same method.

In conclusion, I tried three times, but failed.

The taste and aroma of alcohol were not bad, but Chaeju was too hard. As I should have noticed at first, the rice grains were not fully fermented and when I Chaeju the third K-Sool, the rice grains were still there or even hard. The root of the problem was not heeding the advice that Nuruk should be

fully activated and used. I should have woken up at least Seolhwagog enough, but it seems to have become more of a problem if I didn't.

Although I failed to make K-Sool continuously, it helped me understand more about the characteristics of Seolhwagog. And although it was a bit unreasonable, it became an opportunity to purchase a dedicated Dolora.(I heard later, but it seems that it is not easy to make it properly because there is a saying that if you make alcohol several times, the old taste of alcohol will come out.)

5 inch Dolora
|

If I were to pick the most expensive brewing tool I own, it would be the Dolora. It cost 1.6 million won in cash, but it was an item I always wanted.

Since I don't farm rice, I can't help with rice, but I wanted to try the entire process of making K-Sool on my own. Even though the owner of the mill used to be good at betting rice flour, there was always an unsatisfactory part. I always thought how great it would be to be able to use it at the time I want, in the thickness I want. In addition, it is possible to make K Sool using various grains as well as rice, so I looked around to see which machine would be good.

At first, I didn't know what to buy, so I reviewed various things. Soybean milk machine, grinder, millstone, noodle making machine,, blender, etc. I wanted to have soybean milk machine after seeing it used in the traditional Nuruk school class at the Korean Traditional Fermentation

Academy. However, in the case of the horizontal type, I immediately gave up after seeing reviews saying that the millstone grater does not wear out evenly and that stone powder is crucially smeared.

All grinders and mixers are for drying, so they are not suitable for producing wet rice flour, so they gave up. By the way, I didn't know about the blender until I bought it like a fool, and now it's quietly enshrined in one corner of the house.

The noodle making machine was the most likely tool among them, but it was not suitable for making a lot of rice flour because it was only a manual type for home use. I found out later, but there is an automatic noodle making machine used in Chinese restaurants. It takes some time to grind, but it seems to work well, and looking at the blog of a teacher from the Korea Gayangju Research Institute who is running a K-Sool education center, he bought it used for 300,000 won and used it for 5 years, so it seems to be a strong alternative.

In the meantime, I went to take a beer making class at 'Soma' located under the Korea Gayangju Research Institute and saw the '5-inch Dolora' of Poongjin Food Machinery. I ordered it right away without looking around when I was told that it was not too big and could use 220V power, so it was suitable for a workshop or home use. At first, I was worried about how to use this, but after using it a few times, I got used to it and laughed at how I used to carry rice flour.

In case it helps, here's a summary of how to buy and use a 5-inch Dolora. To purchase, call Poongjin Food Machinery. It tells you your account number as if you are used to it, but if you make a deposit and leave your address, it will be sent by courier(?) right away. If you want help with installation and use, you can pay an additional 100,000 won, but in my case, I did not choose it.

Poongjin Food Machinery 5-inch Dolora

When using it, there is nothing particularly difficult as long as you pay attention to the distance between Dolora. There are two levers in front, but they must be turned at the same time, and the degree of rotation is different, so you can turn it while looking at the interval.

In my case, I tend to make fine rice flour, but the first time, I break the rice grains with a slight gap, and the second time, when I close the distance(do not tighten the lever, just attach it to each other), it comes down very finely.(After using it, turn off the power while leaving enough space between them.)

At first, there are oil stains here and there on Dolora, so throw away some rice and run it once or twice to get rid of it. You can put your hand in and wipe it off, but I don't think you need to worry too much as the rice powder dries and nature falls off over time. However, there is noise and vibration, so it would be better to avoid using it early in the morning or late in the evening.(My wife was so worried about it, so I put a dustproof mat on it, and thanks to that, I took a breath from worrying about noise.)

Seolhwagog Deos-sul Timing Matters

The rice flour problem, though costly, had a complete and satisfactory solution. Next, we had to solve the Seolhwagog Deos-sul timing problem.

First, I asked Director Ryu In-soo. The summary of the director's words is as follows. "Seolhwagog is a natural microorganism and has little power. Because it is rice flour, it emits carbon dioxide well (it does not swell significantly). Seoul Takju also deos-sul in 5 to 7 days. It is good to periodically measure the frequency of Mitsul. Or try estimating through weight change. It's in context with understanding the nature of my Nuruk."

I asked the same question to Park Seon-yeong, head of Kooksoondang, by e-mail.

"Chief Park Sun-young.(Omitted) To be specific, 500g of nonglutinous rice powder is made into Beombeog using 1L of boiling water, and after adding about 1.5kg of rice heut-im Nuruk, about 1L of water is added to make Mitsul. Of course, it takes time for the rice cake-like Mitsul to dissolve, but the problem is that carbon dioxide continues to be generated and bubbling continues after it has been released to some extent. Last year, 5 days in late summer, 7 or 8 days

Seonyoung Park, Head of Kooksoondang Production Headquarters
@Suldoc homepage capture

in autumn, and in winter(room temperature is around 22 degrees), 10 days have passed as of today, and it seems to be still fermenting. I couldn't decide whether I should wait or do Deos-sul now, so I'm asking."

The following is part of Park's reply.

When Deos-sul is made when high-quality yeast is not yet active and the lactic acid bacteria in Mitsul remain inactive, lactic acid bacteria become the dominant species and the K-Sool goes rancid. In the case of rice heut-im Nuruk, Deos-sul is somewhat late because the saccharification power is weak compared to wheat Nuruk and the nutrients are not sufficient. In the case of Ihwaju using Ihwagog(rice) (water supply rate 50%), ferment at 20°C for 7 to 15 days, and when it smells of alcohol and is sufficiently released, make Deos-sul."

Through the words of the two of you, it was confirmed that at least 5 days are required for Seolhwagog to be sufficiently activated, and it was found that Deos-sul is the right thing to do when it is sufficiently released.

But at that moment, suddenly, the thought of how to use the koji crossed my mind.

Koji is also rice heut-im Nuruk, but how is it used?

Koji, Jumo and Moromi
|

My curiosity about the timing of Seolhwagog Deos-sul led to my curiosity about Koji, the same rice heut-im Nuruk, even though the purpose was different, and finally I came to the idea of how sake is made. Sake is made by fermenting rice, so it is made like K-Sool Takju, and it is sold after filtering, heating, and adding water to it.

The details, such as the high rice shaving rate, washing time in seconds, and strict moisture absorption rate, are Japanese and beyond imagination, but in the big picture, the initial process of brewing sake, such as rice polishing, washing, soaking, and Godubap steaming, does not look much different from K-Sool. Afterwards, there is a difference between the production of Koji for saccharification and the production of Jumo using dedicated yeast. Koji is completed over two days by sprinkling Hwanggukgyun in a Nuruk room at a temperature of 35 degrees, and Jumo for pure cultivation of strong yeast takes two weeks or one month. It seems that the reason for the sufficient time is for low temperature fermentation, and it will probably finish sooner if the product temperature is high.

Made Jumo increases the rice input ratio through a three-step sake brewing process, usually at a ratio of 1:2:4.(For some reason, it reminds me of K-Sool Samyangju.) After the final soaking (Deos-sul), fermented at 8-18 degrees for about 3 weeks, moromi, a fermented liquor with a temperature of 18-20 degrees, is completed. Squeeze it out and filter it to make sake.

Seolhwagog Jumo

It was understood that Koji was made and used like Ssias-sul through a process called Jumo, but there was no exact ratio of Koji, yeast, rice, and water. When considering various data, after making Koji, it was summarized that after making it, it was activated by pouring about 1.5 times as much water and used for a week, and about 33% of the amount of rice was used.

Seolhwagog Jumo is boiling

If I match this part to Seolhwagog, it seems that Deos-sul will be easy and easy to manage if I use it after waking it up enough to add about 1.5 times more water than putting it in the mitsul from the beginning and striking it hard.

Based on the fact that Seolhwagog must first be activated using Jumo and the yeast must be proliferated enough by brewing several times, the recipe is decided more systematically. In the meantime, it had to be easy to select and apply the main or sub-materials, and there had to be no problem of insufficient saccharification in continuous brewing.

Seolhwagog Oyangju
|

While studying sake, I was able to find out where so many different flavors of sake come from, and it helped me a lot to come up with my own recipe using Seolhwagog. It is largely divided into three categories: raw material, manufacturing, and finishing. In the raw material part, the flavor varies depending on the brewing rice, rice polishing rate, brewing water, and yeast. Jujumi is literally the rice used for making sake.

Category	Flavor Defference Point	Detail
Raw materia	Differnece according to brewing rice	Differences in flavor according to various types of Japanese sake-making rice(Yamadanishiki, Gohyakumangoku, Miyamanitiki, Omachi, etc.)
	Difference according to rice polishing rate	The taste changes depending on the ratio of shaving the rice (80%, 70%, 55%, 40%, etc.)
	Difference according to brewing water	Hard water gives a sense of body, and soft water gives a soft and voluptuous feeling.

Category	Flavor Defference Point	Detail
Manufacturing	Difference according to yeast	Provided by the Japan Association Using yeast of various Brewing Yeast flavors(No. 6, No. 7, No. 9, No. 14, No.15, etc.)
	Difference according to Jumo	Differences in wine quality according to the method of adding lactic acid bacteria (cultivation of natural lactic acid bacteria, addition of lactic acid, etc.)
	Differences according to Cheju	Differences in taste depending on which part of the sake is taken (first, middle, last, etc.)
	Difference by filtration	Flavor difference according to the degree of filtration (normal filtration, no filtration, etc.)
Finishing	Difference according to heating (sterilization)	Flavor difference according to heating time, whether or not heated, and number of times(2 times before storage/shipment, 1 time before storage, 1 time before shipment, no heat treatment, etc.)
	Difference according to ripening	Flavor difference according to release time (spring release, fall release, release after aging for more than 3 years, etc.)

Sake Flavor Elements [16]

As mentioned in the basic ingredients of K-Sool, the difference between nonglutinous rice and glutinous rice, specifically the difference in rice variety, can make the basic flavor of sake different.

Rice milling ratio and water use do not seem to have much meaning personally, and there is no direct correlation between yeast and K-Sool using Nuruk. However, since the characteristics of Seolhwagog differ depending on the main ingredient, sub-material(juice), and seed nuruk used when making Seolhwagog, separating and developing the types in that respect will affect the flavor.

From a manufacturing point of view, depending on how much delay the production of Jumo or Mitsul is, it seems that there will be a difference in the degree of acidity caused by lactic acid bacteria. And, in the process of brewing sake, sake is classified in detail according to the method of brewing and the point of acquisition, and these parts seem to be sufficiently applicable to K-Sool.

In addition, the difference in filtration, heating, and aging will affect the flavor without saying anything, but the relationship is not great from the point of view of facility constraints and microorganisms living in K-Sool.

While pondering over and over again, the Korea Gayangju Research Institute Oyangju recipe caught my eye.

It was good that the yeast was multiplied twice(three times with Jumo) and Nuruk split to help saccharify. Deos-sul materials and processing methods can be different. In particular, dividing Godubap is a way to maximize the fermentation effect, and since the first Godubap and the second Godubap ingredients can be used differently, it can be transformed into various forms. The capacity of the steamer I have can make 4 kg of Godubap at a time, so I envisioned the recipe as follows.(Note that the first Godubap is glutinous rice and the second is nonglutinous rice)

		Rice	Water	Nuruk	Flour	Method	Remark
	Jumo		2.0	1.3		1.5 times water	Seolhwagog
6 days later	Mitsul	0.5	1.0	Jumo	0.2	Beombeog	Add Jumo
3 days later	Does-sul1	1.0	2.0			Beombeog	
3 days later	Does-sul2	1.0	2.0	0.7		Beombeog	Add Seolhwagog
3 days later	Does-sul3	2.0				Glutinous Godubap	Add the divided Godubap
7 days later	Does-sul4	2.0	2.0			Non-Glutinous Godubap	After filtering Does-sul3
	Total	6.5	7.0	2.0	0.2		
	Ratio	1.0	1.1	30%	3%	← Relative to the amount of rice	

Standard Oyangju recipe using Seolhwagog Jumo (flour optional)

I liked the recipe very much. From now on, it is Oyangju.

Let's call it Seolhwa-Oyangju.

K-Sool Competition Challenge ④

Yeoju Five Grain Brewed
Gayangju Evaluation Contest, 2022

It is a new competition created in 2021. In the first year, I couldn't participate because of the late information, and in the second year, I had a secret weapon called Seolhwagog, so I prepared with great effort. They had to use Yeoju rice sent by the organizers and submit at least 10 photos of the process of using it. Sweet potatoes, including purple sweet potatoes, are specified as secondary ingredients, it seems that Yeoju is famous for its sweet potatoes.

I was wondering if I could get extra points, and the color would be fine if I used purple sweet potato, so I used sweet potato instead of Oyangju's last non-glutinous rice Godubap. One thing to pay attention to is the moisture content of the sub-material. Sweet potato has 60% water content. In other words, 10kg of sweet potato actually contains 4kg of starch and 6kg of water.

You have to take this into consideration when designing your recipe. Sweet potatoes were washed, peeled, and steamed like Godubap.

Made with Oyangju, and having already split Godubap in the third Deossul, the sweet potato was fully fermented when opened for Chaeju. Calculated by the amount of grain, the sweet potato is about 24%, but after filtering the alcohol, the color was too dark and the

taste of sweet potato was felt, so I wondered if I added too much.

I borrowed even my wife's name and submitted it to both categories, Takju and Yakju. Fortunately, both passed the preliminary round, but looking at the entries in the final round, I had an ominous feeling because mine was the only entry using sweet potatoes. A bad hunch is never wrong. When I went to Yeoju and came back empty-handed, I felt very depressed, but it seemed clear that the use of unfamiliar sweet potatoes as a secondary ingredient was the cause of the drop. It was a moment to engrave the ordinary truth that what looks vaguely good is not good, but what is definitely good through hands-on experience.(Bye, sweet potato~)

Korea Gayangju Research Institute Gungjungsul Competetion, 2020(Gwahaju)

The Gungjungsul Brewing Contest is a K-Sool contest hosted by the Korea Gayangju Research Institute. Looking at the contents of 'suldoc.com' on the Korea Gayangju Research Institute website, it seems that the first contest was held in 2012, so it has already been more than 10 years.

Gungjungsul is the liquor brewed in the palace for offerings to the king or for state events, and it is said that it was planned with the purpose of promoting Korea's high-quality liquor and liquor brewing culture. The way each competition presents a new theme is unique. There were K-Sool by flower, lotus leaf, grain, Nuruk and Gwahaju. In particular, in 2018, the Ihwaju Live Contest was held at COEX, and it is said that they showed a unique scene of brewing K-Sool with their own Ihwagog on the spot.(It must have been sweaty to mix and blend Nuruk)

The theme for the first year of participation was Gwahaju. The original Gwahaju of the port wine type, in which distilled spirit is added during fermentation, is also good, but I wanted to make a sherry wine-type Gwahaju that uses a special distilled spirit in the fermented liquor. I asked the director in advance if it was possible, and he said it was okay, so I continued.

Summarizing the manufacturing method written in the application form, saengju(liquor with ginger) is first sweetened (rice:water ratio is 1:0.8), and then distilled saeanju is mixed at a ratio of 2:1. And El Dorado, American hops, are dry-hopped and adjusted alcohol degree to 25. It seems that they  were expecting a somewhat strong dry liquor with a subtle ginger scent and a citrus hop scent.

Looking at the blog at the time, it seems that the taste and aroma were not satisfactory, contrary to expectations, but now that I think about it, it seems that the alcohol was too high and the taste and aroma were not properly expressed.

Anyway, with a swollen heart, I took it to Bangbae-dong and submitted it, but was unfortunately dropped. For the Gungjungsul Competetion, I can receive the results of the screening if I wish, but it seems it doen't that was the case at this time. Exactly what was lacking is still a mystery. Korea Gayangju Research Institute Gungjungsul Competetion,

2021(Yeon-yeobju)

The second year, Yeon-yeobju was the subject. Lotus leaves are easy to obtain and have many uses as a secondary ingredient. When making Yeon-yeoju, I always worry about how many lotus leaves to put in. I visited the Folk Village in Oeam-ri, Asan, because there is Yeon-yeoju, designated as an intangible cultural property of Chungcheongnam-do. When I came out with the brown Yeon-yeoju in a plastic bottle, I thought it was a bit shabby compared to its reputation, but I remember being surprised at how sour it tasted. (I salivate just thinking about it.) Anyway, Asan Yeon-yeoju uses 4-5 lotus leaves in a 10L pot. I tried to follow along, but looking at my blog history at the time, it seems that it wasn't very good.

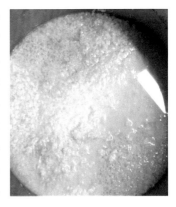

"When I scooped the clear liquor above, the rice was in a state of sinking a lot, but the liquor was not clear as a whole, and it did not look good as it was cloudy and had floating substances in a dark yellow form. It seems to have a weak lotus leaf scent, but it is not greatly felt due to the scent of Glutinous rice alcohol. It is too sweet, and the vigor of the lotus leaf is weak. However, at the end of the drink, there is a lotus leaf vigor that seems to be spicy. Overall, it is too sweet and strong hides other flavors and aromas and is incompatible. Consider diluting and bottling separately, or boldly distilling to increase the value."

I remembered the sentence 'Too much is as bad as too little'. As in the previous Gwahaju, the taste and aroma are made too strong, so the whole is not harmonious. I decided to reduce the amount of lotus leaf used and make it a little lighter.

The actual entry used two pieces, one for steam Godubap and one for Deos-sul. 'Seolhwagog scent, soft texture, dry overall, and lotus leaf scent subtly permeated' was written at the time of Chaeju, so the balance was not bad. However, it seemed too dry, so I added the sweet K-Sool I had prepared and slightly adjusted the taste. But conclusion is drop out.

The 2021 competition sent the screening results when requested. The overall average score was not in the middle of the ranking. Judging from the fact that it is on the poor side in terms of balance in the score classification, and the judges' evaluation opinions are 'it feels slightly bland' and 'it seems that water has been added, and the taste is half-halved as a result', it seems that the addition of water in the last step was poisonous. I thought it couldn't be done this way. Instead of adapting myself to the competition, my personality needs to be projected into the competition as it is. Over-painting that does not suit is because it makes me confused whether the dropout is due to my skills or the wrong addition.

Part 5

Now, Going to Brew

I have my own Nuruk and a recipe using it. Now it's time to make KSool in earnest, but I'm deeply concerned about what kind of K-Sool it should be. I organize my experience during that time to see what color, taste, and scent I am pursuing and how to incorporate it into my K-Sool.

My K-Sool Color,
Colorful brightness or clarity

The tongue only touches, the eyes taste first

|

While experimenting with various Seolhwagog, I realized how important the color of K-Sool is. No matter how good the taste and scent are, if the color is dark or there are floating particles, the interest decreases. It's a fact I learned while studying, but it's because our human vision is more developed than our sense of taste or smell. (Half of our brain is used for visual information processing.) In other words, 'good-looking rice cakes are also good to eat' and 'the tongue only touches, the eyes taste first.'

This is something that has been learned from humanity's long history of gathering and hunting, and the reason why people avoid blue food and prefer red food is because blue food is rare in nature and well-ripened fruit is mostly red. Here are two interesting experiments.

When coffee was poured into a blue, transparent, or white cup, the coffee in the transparent or white cup had a strong scent and bitter taste, but the blue cup did not. The reason is that in the case of a transparent or white cup, the coffee color appears vividly and recognizes its inherent bitterness, but in the case of a blue cup, it softens the brown concentration and feels less bitter.

Another similar example is that when red pigment is added to white wine, it tastes like red wine, so it's no exaggeration to say that the eyes change the taste.[17] Therefore, although the taste and scent of K-Sool are important, how it looks is more important and there are various factors such as bottle shape and color, cap, label, glass etc., but I would like to think about K-Sool color and transparency first.

K-Sool color

The color of K-Sool can also be linked to its identity. Choi Haeng-suk's traditional liquor 'Ahwangju' has a name that means yellow goose down feathers in itself, and it has been praised for its not to much sweetness and proper acidity as well as its clean aftertaste that goes well with its color. Recently released 'Gold (GOLD)' takes gold as its motif as its name suggests. As you know, gold represents success, achievement, victory and an unchanging image. The sparkling clear golden color raises the value of K-Sool to its fullest. It has been released for a while now but when it comes to K-Sool color you can't miss Sulsam's 'Drunk Monkey'. It has a deep red hue due to being brewed with red mold on Hongguk rice and has been loved for a long time along with its unique label design(Sulsaem CEO Shin In-geon said it was something he did while drinking in college…).

It has a unique visual appeal and is definitely one of the most popular home party products along with Makgeolli. If you look at the colors of different types of K-Sool, in the case of rice Makgeolli it should be 'white and clean' in color and in the case of wheat Makgeolli it should have a 'light ivory' color. If it is different or ripe you need to see what kind of influence the ingredients and Nuruk had. Clear liquor (Cheongju) should be 'clear and transparent' as its name suggests and the best Cheongju has a 'light and transparent light greenish hue'.

The fact that blue light comes from K-Sool means that fresh and good rice was used. Especially if there are no impurities or fine dust it will be worth more[18] as much so I thought it was an important point.

I mentioned Seolhwagog several times when talking about Seolhwagog but once the K-Sool color is dark I lose interest myself. It is good sweetening power and fermentation power but only when it can produce the desired color.

Therefore you need to be very careful when using Nuruk and if you see white mold on Seolhwagog surface you should move on to the next step immediately to prevent unnecessary spore or mold generation.

Even when using general market wheat Nuruk you need to use Ssias-sul or increase Deos-sul times to minimize the amount so that you can reduce the 'yellowish color' that wheat has. Of course squeezing out wheat flour is natural.

Once Nuruk control is done you need to look at your main ingredient rice.

Of course you should use new rice instead of faded old rice and wash it carefully with care to remove impurities such as dirt oil protein etc from its surface so that rice's inherent color can be expressed. It is possible to keep the amount of rice left after shaving like sake below 60%, but soaking the rice in water for a long time can also be a good method.

It is called 'Sanjang' and if you soak rice in water for a long time natural microorganisms (lactic acid bacteria) will remove the protein from rice and make alcohol that is rich in scent and has a creamy smooth and clean taste[19] . According to Park Seon-young head of Kooksoondang our ancestors used microorganisms to shave rice more delicately instead of polishing it.

You can see holes on the surface of the rice.
@ Capture from the patent 'Method for manufacturing fermented rice wine with improved fragrance and stability'

There are also many differences in color depending on the type of rice.

Non-glutinous rice alcohol on the top left, Glutinous rice alcohol on the right, mixed below (the difference in alcohol color is clear.)

Non-glutinous rice is darker than Glutinous rice and Glutinous rice is darker than brown rice. (Black rice goes without saying) So if you're chasing good K-Sool color you should mainly use Non-glutinous rice and if you need beautiful golden color you should make a recipe centered around Glutinous rice.

I once visited Songdohyang Korea traditional liquor brewery and when Kang Hak-mo CEO asked me to taste it the color of the K-Sool was very light red and looked very good. When I asked how this color came out he said he added a little black rice. Songdohyang is known for making dry K-Sool mainly with Non-glutinous rice but adding a little red to it made it look even more luxurious.

Adding color

It's enough with just rice, water, and Nuruk, but there are times when you want to create a special color. In this case, you can put 30-50g of freeze-dried powder ingredients with color per 10kg of rice in the final stage of K-Sool completion. Depending on the color, there are gardenia(yellow with a reddish hue), jicho/omija/purple sweet potato(red), turmeric(yellow), baekryeoncho(light purple), paprika(red/orange/yellow/green), black rice(black), etc., and you can easily find them by using internet shopping.

Although we are talking about K-Sool color, how clear it is(transparency) is also a very important factor. Especially for our clear liquo (Cheongju). (It's not called Cheongju for nothing.) Let's think about filtration next.

Low temperature sedimentation filteration

Everyone who brews alcohol wants to have crystal clear K-Sool. However, there is not much that a beginner can do for this. The easiest is low temperature sedimentation filtration. I found a well-explained passage on the 'Goljagnara Research Institute' blog(owner: Sumjingang Nuruk Flower) by chance.[20]

"The most delicious K-Sool is filtered with a difference in pressure caused by the weight of the undiluted solution itself, without applying any pressure. And it is a pure and clear liquor naturally filtered with 'Yongsu'. If you store the K-Sool filtered with water at 0~4 degrees, the protein and other substances in the alcohol will condense and settle to the bottom, and the clear alcohol will rise to the top. If the sugar content of the alcohol is high and the viscosity is strong, so that no precipitation occurs, you can lower the viscosity by diluting it with water after precipitating it at room temperature and then keeping it at low temperature, but there is a disadvantage that the alcohol content decreases."

After squeezing two kinds of alcohol and putting them in the refrigerator (left), the degree of precipitation over time (middle, right). The speed and degree vary depending on the characteristics of alcohol.

In other words, if you squeeze out alcohol and store it in a refrigerator, clear alcohol will accumulate over time. If you do this several times by scooping it out and transferring it, you can get very clear alcohol. It is a widely used method even in small breweries, and if you have to pick a bad point, it takes a long time and requires a large refrigerator capacity.

It would be good to know briefly about the sedimentation speed. The faster the sedimentation speed, the more water there is, the lower the degree, the less sweet, the lower the temperature, and the more

flour used based on experience. There are always people who ask when they bring well-settled clear K-Sool.

"How can K-Sool be so clear?"

Then I usually say this.

"Some things just take time."

Filter press filteration

But people can't always be leisurely, and when Yakju is needed at the right time, they can't just roll their feet in front of the refrigerator. Let me introduce an interesting episode. In 2019 Gayangju Brewer Selection Competition, I had to submit 6L of Yakju brewed with Gyeonggi Cham Dream Non-glutinous rice, but I was clumsy at handling Non-glutinous rice and had Chaeju in just one month because of a short submission period when it usually took more than two months. The time to send was approaching…

No matter how much I measured it, it was only about 5L at most, so I quickly looked for a filtration method and what caught my eye was filter press filtration.

It is usually used for wine filtration, but when I went to <Yes Wine> because there was a small one, it was as much as 770,000 won.(It's now 990,000 won!) Should I buy it even if it's expensive because I'll keep using it later? Can I use it well if I buy it without knowing how to use it? While hesitating like this, I found out about a company that  imports related equipment in Korea and called them recklessly. "You… are you an importer of small filters? Can you filter my K Sool just once? I'll pay you." The other party was silent for a moment and then said "Yes. It's possible. But since filter paper is a consumable item and we have to clean it after use. You have to give us 250,000 won."

The filter machine is 770,000 won, but for filtering once 250,000 won… Cleanly gave up and gave up on submission as well.(If I had put even water to match 6L… Sometimes I have useless thoughts.) Later on watching filter press filtration usage or videos made me think that I did well not to buy them. It seemed difficult to use at home little by little as careful pumping speed control was necessary and if pressing was slightly loose, alcohol would leak out from top to bottom.

Vacuum filteration

I gave up on filter press filtration but not on my desire for filtration. The solution to this problem was found unexpectedly close by. It was at Korea Gayangju Research Institute's last class of owner class where vacuum filtration practice was held. The vacuum filtration method that seems to have come from chemical experiments is 'a form of suction by manipulating the pressure inside the filter paper lower than atmospheric pressure', simply put, sucking out only clear

alcohol with a vacuum pump. After filter press filtration, I thought it was an excellent opportunity and recorded all classes that day without missing any classes and bought all components used for filtration. It cost a total of 720000 won(of which vacuum pump was 480000 won), but thinking about it now is almost same with filter press filtration machine price. In case anyone is interested in vacuum filtration, here are some components needed for configuration.

Guest vacuum pump(※Caution: Be sure to plug into a valve with '-' value. If plugged in reverse…), three-way flask 3L with branches (for receiving clear liquor), Buchner funnel inner diameter 150mm, ADVANTECK quantitative filter paper No. 2/150mm, Buchner flask rubber gasket 6pieces, three-way flask 1L with branches(for vacuum trap, prevents alcohol from flowing back), vacuum tube No.8(inner diameter 8mm), filter diatomaceous earth, etc.

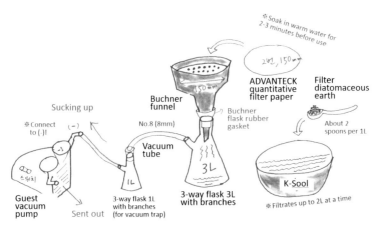

Vacuum filtration overall configuration

The overall configuration can be referred to the configuration diagram up, and as mentioned earlier, be careful of the valve position of the vacuum pump. Diatomaceous earth is enough to put about 2 spoons per liter, and filter paper is soaked in warm water for 2-3 minutes

before use to remove impurities, remove paper smell, and improve adhesion. The capacity of the flask that receives clear alcohol is 3L, but there is a branch in the middle, so it should be stopped when it exceeds a little over 2L.If you are greedy for a moment, there is a risk of backflow.(If backflow occurs, alcohol enters the pump…

If you filter it, the taste and aroma will be slightly lost. Some people like it better and some don't. In my case, the flavor is weak, so it's closer to the non-side. Unless it is used as a contest entry or gift, lowtemperature sedimentation filtration seems to be sufficient.

Millstone filteration(aka. Weight lifting filteration)

To close the article, there is a filtering method that is a good idea but has not been tried in practice, so I will add it. It's called millstone filtration, and while I was looking for information on Hosanchun in Mungyeong, I came across a picture of Hosanchun filtering with a millstone in an article.

Indeed, I remembered what Shim Hyung-seok, director of the Korean Liquor Research Institute, said during the Korea Gayangju Research Institute leadership class.

Captured from <Park Soon-wook's K-Sool Tour (69)>

"The method of weaving by hand stretches the fabric and ferment escapes, and it takes a lot of force and has very low efficiency. Instead, if you use a microfiber net and place a very heavy object on top to let it slowly filter naturally, you can get better results. It should wwwwIn the same context, there are similar cases among the Korea Gayangju Research Institute cafe articles, and there are tips that you can use weights or dumbbells if you do not have a millstone, so please refer to them.

So what about my K-Sool?

Seolhwagog is 100% rice Nuruk, which helps to bring out the original color of the main ingredient. The fact that wheat hulls were not mixed in was a great advantage. It is also easy to make a special color. When making Nuruk, it can be made by mixing colored grains, and it can also be used at the appropriate Deos-sul point during the Oyangju manufacturing process.

The color I want is a colorful bright color. If I look back at the process of that time, the color of the K-Sool should not be dark under any circumstances. Even when adding color, it should be applied very lightly and subtly. If it is thick, it may give the drinker an unintended feeling. That feeling may be the feeling of wanting to drink, but I don't think it's from my experience so far.

Takju, of course, should be white, and when making yakju, it is important to filter it at low temperature for as long as possible to obtain a clear alcohol. If additional filtration is necessary to add value and the amount is 5. Now, Going to Brew 207 not large, as discussed, vacuum filtration is considered the best method.

My K-Sool taste,
harmonious without being sweet

Change in taste

|

Before talking about the taste of K-Sool, it would be better to discuss the taste first. As food scientist Choi Nak-eon said, 'Taste reflects all human desires,' taste has roots and as desires change slightly over time, the preferred taste also changes. When I first stepped into society in 1989, Makgeolli was sour and had a heavy sour taste. (That's why we all hated it.) The closest taste now would be Geumjeongsanseong Makgeolli, and the biggest difference from other market Makgeollis besides using selfmade Nuruk is that it does not use aspartame. As you know, aspartame is an artificial sweetener that is 200 times sweeter than sugar and dominated the world with permission from the National Tax Service in 1991.

The most dramatic change in taste may be sourness.

When I first started brewing K-Sool in 2016, if alcohol had a sour taste, it was considered a bad alcohol(acidification) where lactic acid bacteria proliferated excessively or aged. However, when Yangju-do's 'ByeolsanMakgeolli' won the highest award at the 2020 Korean Liquor Awards, it opened up a new world of sourness(acidity).

ByeolsanMakgeolli and vinegar bacteria
@<ParkSoon-wook's K-Sool Journey (23)> Capture

ByeolsanMakgeolli adds vinegar bacteria during early fermentation to maximize sourness. This change in taste even lifted regulations such as a total acidity of 0.5%.(The name Byeolsan itself means 'special sourness'.)

I want to give an example that shows that sourness is the trend.

I analyze the winning works of K-Sool competitions every year and the analysis results of the 2021 winning works were interesting. In the Takju category out of a total of 14 alcohols most of the winning works were light alcohols with an alcohol content of less than 16 degrees(mine was 17.2 degrees) and my alcohol acidity was the lowest at 0.31% along with another alcohol with the same acidity and received an encouragement award together.(The encouragement award is the lowest award.)

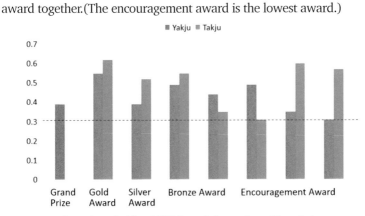

Comparison of acidity of 2021 Gayangju Brewer Competition winning works (the last Yakju encouragement award is me.)

The alcohols that received higher awards than me were generally high in sugar and acidity so in one word they were alcohols with strong sweetness and acidity.(Interestingly the alcohol that received the gold medal had an alcohol content of 11.8 degrees a sugar content of 23.3 Brix and the highest acidity of 0.62%. It is expected to be very light but also very sweet and also a new sour alcohol.)

How will alcohol taste change in the future? What kind of alcohol taste should I pursue?

Sweet taste

K-Sool is basically sweet. Director Park Rok-dam of Korea Traditional Liquor Research Institute said in <Rewriting Jubangmun> "The Gayangju that our ancestors enjoyed by brewing themselves were completely different from today's alcohol taste very sweet and soft and as a directional liquor with deep scent like flowers or fruits from alcohol brewed only with rice and Nuruk. It is not such alcohol that gets drunk quickly by drinking only a little like today's alcohol with high alcohol content."

Perhaps sugar was more precious than it is now and women who led Gayangju culture preferred sweetness more than men. In addition it would have been advantageous for storage and preservation from a sweet perspective. Director Park said that because our old people had drinking habits and culture to enjoy unique flavors while drinking little naturally they had a sweet form that could not be drunk all at once. It seemed like an insight worthy of a master who restored hundreds of K-Sools.

Looking back at the process of brewing alcohol it seems relatively easy to make it sweet. There are two main ways: first using more rice compared to water. If the basic recipe is rice:water 1:1 then even if it is 1:0.8 very sweet alcohol is made.(A representative example is Seogtanju which is hard to swallow.) This is because if the alcohol content exceeds a certain level fermentation no longer occurs and the remaining sugar accumulates as residual sugar making it

sweet. An extreme example is Dongjeongchun. Dongjeongchun which produces one bottle per field has a rice:water ratio of 11:1 which is almost like rice honey so it's very sweet and its price reaches 500000 won per bottle.

Another way is to intentionally suppress alcohol fermentation during brewing. Representative examples are Dongyangju, Cheongmyeongju etc. which are mixed when Godubap is hot during Godubap Deos-sul. In this case the yeast dies at high temperature and the alcohol becomes low in alcohol content but sweet.

Or you can raise the product temperature to kill the yeast, which is called 'bosam' which wraps the container with blankets to raise the temperature. Similarly the alcohol is low in alcohol content but sweet.(For reference product temperature refers to the innermost temperature of the alcohol barrel.)

One thing to note about sweetness is that not all sweetness is the same even if it's sweet. As mentioned when explaining rice the more amylose content the more not sticky and the more amylopectin content the more sticky it is. Therefore Glutinous rice alcohol has a loose starch structure that is easily destroyed and quickly saccharified but grape sugar chains in split parts are not well decomposed and remain as nonfermentable sugar. This leads to body sensation and sticky sweetness. On the other hand if Non-glutinous rice is brewed even if it is sweet it feels clean and light. I think Non-glutinous rice alcohol is still a high-grade sweetness.

Director An Dam-yoon of Naol Dam Brewery who first helped me with K-Sool brewing had a theory that 'alcohol for accompaniment should not be sweet' and released dry alcohol as he wished. "It may be somewhat difficult for the general public who like sweetness but it has the charm of being able to empty a bottle at once with food as an accompaniment." Even without quoting Representative Lee Ji-min of Daedong Yeojudo I think that the position of sweet alcohol continues to decrease and unless it is very extreme not sweet very dry or harmonious with other tastes such an atmosphere will be created.

Personally I don't like sweet alcohol but depending on where alcohol is needed there are times when sweetness is needed. In that case, if you make very sweet alcohol with less water using Glutinous rice Mitsul and Glutinous rice Deos-sul, and keep only the clear alcohol in the fridge, you can blend it as much as you need when you need it.

Sour taste

According to a paper published in a philosophical journal by Robert Dunn, a professor from North Carolina in the United States, and others, sourness is called the 'lost taste' because it has been almost unexplored compared to other tastes. This is because while sweetness indicates calories, umami indicates protein, saltiness indicates essential salt components of the body, and bitterness indicates the presence of toxic components, it is unclear what sourness means. Researchers speculate that this may be because the common ancestor of primates and humans lost the ability to synthesize vitamin C 60-70 million years ago. Yeast and lactic acid bacteria during the fermentation process increase the calorie content and increase the amino acid and vitamin content. As a result, people are naturally drawn to sour tastes, but I'm not sure.

The recent sourness craze seems more convincing in the words of food scientist Choi Nak-eon. "Sourness itself is not very attractive. It's also a sign of spoiled food. However, when combined with other tastes (usually sweetness), it enhances the taste and aroma." In addition, sourness is also an excellent stimulant, so when I think of a sour taste, my mouth waters.

I couldn't find any specific evidence, but I heard that when per capita income reaches $30,000, preferences shift from sweetness to sourness. I think it reflects the atmosphere of pursuing individuality from quantity to quality and from survival issues.

As I mentioned at the beginning, I learned alcohol during a time when sourness was avoided and personally did not like sourness, so it was difficult to give acidity to alcohol. Especially since the trend in major KSool competitions was to require moderate acidity. For example, like this.

"Your K-Sool is really delicious. But I think it would be better if there was some acidity."

Eventually I confided my worries to Director Ryu In-soo and he gave me a wise answer.

"People who talk about K-Sool taste respond based on some K-Sool they have tasted before. If your K-Sool matches that, it will just be one of many K-Sools. Rather than chasing ordinary known K-Sool, wouldn't it be better to focus more on my own K-Sool that I like?" (Of course I couldn't say anything. Should I say it hit me right in the bones?)

Anyway, acidity is an important and necessary element in K-Sool whether large or small. Have you ever seen a sensory evaluation item? There are color, taste and aroma and there must be a sense of balance. It can be a sense of balance for the entire alcohol but a good K-Sool will have balanced umami in terms of taste.

Let's think about how to give acidity to K-Sool.

The easiest way is to increase the amount of water compared to rice. As the amount of water increases, sweetness decreases and other tastes become more prominent and lactic acid bacteria survive more as alcohol content decreases and sourness increases. The Deos-sul point also affects acidity. Usually when Mitsul is done, lactic acid bacteria and acetic acid bacteria that proliferate quickly take their place first and block other bacteria from invading but soon yeast eats sugar and grows rapidly so that when alcohol content reaches 10 degrees or more lactic acid bacteria can no longer use their strength. What if yeast growth is delayed? Probably more acid would have been produced and since produced acid does not disappear it would have acidity in alcohol.

It also looks useful from what I heard on the internet cafe 'People who make alcohol' that I frequent. It can give acidity by reducing the amount of water to make sweet alcohol but delaying Chaeju point. Using the principle that naturally becomes sour over time it can get sweet yet sour taste unlike previous method so it's worth applying.

I talked about Byulsan Makgeolli while talking about taste but like putting separate acetic acid bacteria at an appropriate time during early fermentation K-Sool technique can also use 'Sanjang method' which soaks rice for a long time.

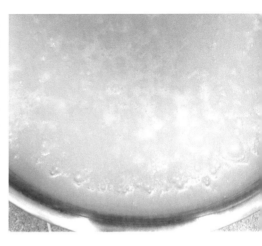

If you soak rice in water for a long time it will slightly soften and pH will decrease so if you make Godubap at this state it will be like putting high-acid raw materials so not only will sourness increase but also rice soaked with tangy scent will later appear as fruit or flower scent giving two birds with one stone effect(left picture of rice soaked for a long time foaming and softening).

In a similar way, there is Sugog, which is used after soaking Nuruk in water.

Acids such as lactic acid are produced during soaking process so when used acidity increases. Usually Danyangju is more sour than Iyangju or Samyangju for this reason.

Bitter taste

Once, before a K-Sool competition, a teacher from a leader class who had won an award before me gave me some advice on the mechanism of winning the competition. First of all, if the K-Sool is bitter, it is a dropout. And he said that if there is some sweetness, the chances of winning increase. While listening to him, I kept thinking of the movie <A Bittersweet Life>. In the original English, it's a 'Bitter but Sweet' life, so why did they translate it into a 'Sweet' life? Is it a box office failure if the movie title is bitter?

Usually people don't like bitterness but like the diverse bitterness of beer, unique bitterness that goes well with other tastes and aromas provides a new experience. Recently, the expression 'little bitter' has been noticed a little in tasting opinions and I am personally glad.

Beer @pixabay.com

Anyway, to be 'little bitter', it must be 'somewhat bitter', so we should avoid alcohol that is too bitter. So when and why does alcohol become bitter? I collected opinions from here and there and added my personal experience to organize cases where alcohol becomes bitter.

1) In case of incomplete fermentation
  - Protein is not completely decomposed and bitterness remains
2) In case of using a lot of Nuruk
  - Yeast itself has a bitter taste and when decomposed after death it leaves a bitter taste
3) In case of fermentation at high temperature - Yeast starts to die at 30 degrees or higher and leaves a bitter taste when decomposed
4) In case of long-term storage of Jigemi
  - Sediment itself is a byproduct of yeast and accompanies amino acid waste
5) In case of high protein content in rice
  - Protein turns into amino acid and some amino acids have a bitter taste
6) In case of rapid fermentation
  - The amount of amino acid increases explosively and strongly feels peptides that produce bitterness

If you look at the cases alone it seems like there is no pattern but if you organize them by cause two keywords stand out. First protein. Rice consists of starch(carbohydrates), protein, fat(lipids), etc. Starch turns into alcohol protein turns into amino acid and lipid turns into aromatic components affecting the flavor of alcohol. Especially during the process of protein turning into amino acid substances(peptides) that produce bitterness are produced so first reducing the amount of protein seems good(choosing rice varieties with low protein content or washing rice more or soaking in water for longer to discharge outside) and when there is bitterness delaying Chaeju or giving time for complete decomposition through cold storage seems necessary.

Next Nuruk. Yeast itself has a bitter taste and leaves a bitter taste when decomposed after death so effort is needed to use less Nuruk and not expose it to high temperature. Basically avoid making alcohol in hot summer and if temperature rises open lid and stir well up and down etc. to keep microorganisms healthy. In case of Takju drink quickly or consume as gift to acquaintance or if you have to keep for long time store only clear alcohol as Cheongju then it will be less likely to become bitter.

Other taste

There is a characteristic taste of grain fermented alcohol which is savory taste. It's an important element in Korean taste but it's the taste that comes from protein being broken down into amino acids. The problem is that this taste becomes stronger as alcohol ages. Like China's famous Sohuang liquor Sohuang Huangju which increases in value as it ages but usually not welcomed as intestinal sound. So drink quickly or remove Jigemi completely and age it.

Lastly I don't know if I can call it a taste but there is a cool taste that is refreshingness. Refreshingness comes from carbon dioxide dissolved in alcohol so it feels stronger at lower temperatures so it's good to drink cold.

So what about my K-Sool?

If you want a glass of alcohol after work sweet would be good but sweet alcohol gets boring quickly. Rather than emphasizing sweetness I want to pursue harmony of various tastes. Seolhwa-Oyangju focuses on nonglutinous rice recipes so rather than being sweet it has light sweetness cannot be ignored. Seolhwa-Oyangju raises acidity by soaking glutinous rice Godubap for Deos-sul3 in Sanjang method. Harmony of non-sweet umami this is the taste of my alcohol that I pursue. overall. Then bitterness and alcohol stimulation can stand out so this part is supplemented by choosing glutinous rice for Deos-sul3.

In addition reflecting recent trends some acidity needs to be given because balance in terms of alcohol is important and public demand cannot be ignored. Seolhwa-Oyangju raises acidity by soaking glutinous rice Godubap for Deos-sul3 in Sanjang method. Harmony of non-sweet umami this is the taste of my alcohol that I pursue.

My K-Sool scent, as much as I want

Garden of the Nile

|

There is an empty perfume bottle
on my office desk. There is no
perfume left, but if you bring your
nose close, you can smell it. 'UN
JARDIN SUR LE NIL', this Hermes
perfume called 'Garden of the Nile'
caught my heart among several
perfumes in the same series when
I first met it on a business trip to
Europe in the early 2000s. The
comfortable floral scent that follows
the cool first scent and the feeling of
being in the middle of a fresh grass
forest as if walking along the Nile

River is just like its name. Above all, this perfume reminds me of my mid-30s when I was full of energy. Vision, taste, hearing, touch, etc. are processed and recognized in the brain, but smell is directly transmitted to the limbic system closest in distance.

This area contains the hippocampus and amygdala which control memory learning and emotions. In other words, the scent we smell rises from some emotion that is remembered deep down before it is interpreted(cognized). This phenomenon also known as the 'Proust effect' is why 'Garden of the Nile' is particularly special to me.

All brewers want their alcohol to have complex scents. But the problem is that they can't explain exactly what kind of scent it should be. It is usually talked about as floral, fruity, honey, citrus, woody, earthy, etc. but it is far from complex beauty. Looking back at the Korea Gayangju Research Institute Korea traditional liquor sommelier course in 2018, the reason why it was difficult especially in terms of scent was that we couldn't express scents we didn't know(didn't experience) and even scents we vaguely knew were difficult to explain. Wine coffee and other fields have already made considerable progress and they have dedicated flavor wheels and aroma kits.

Fortunately, a Korea traditional liquor flavor wheel was developed by the Rural Development Administration in 2019. As introduced by saying 'expressing the taste and scent of our Korea traditional liquor in words that Koreans can easily associate with' it was fortunate and very happy that it was composed of easy words such as freshly cooked rice, mugwort, soy sauce, meju, jipulagi, burnt smell etc. that are melted into our daily lives.(I also look forward to a Korea traditional liquor aroma kit.)

Science of Scent

But just as you need to know English no matter how good Korean is you need to study scents that are commonly understood. I happened to see an interview with Thierry Wasser chief perfumer at Guerlain one of France's oldest perfume companies and it was impressive that he said he needed 'excellent head and physical strength' rather than excellent sense of smell.

"What do you think a perfumer needs most if not an excellent sense of smell?" "Excellent head and physical strength. There are currently about 3,000 basic scents used in perfumery. Perfumers must know them all. Not just knowing, but being able to distinguish and remember each scent anytime anywhere. Only then can you find a solution for how to mix which scents in which order to produce the scent you have drawn in your head. Of course I can do that. Anyway you need a good head for that. In the end a great perfumer is someone who can control processes such as deciding on scents used in manufacturing while abstracting abstract scents drawn in imagination into reality. You need creativity."

If you look around bookstores there aren't many books about scents surprisingly. Scent research may be later than other parts and like it's hard to capture scents it may be hard to confine them in books I think. While doing so I read <Philosophy of Scent> by Hirayama Noriyaki which was very helpful.

In particular organizing scent expressions commonly spoken such as floral, fruity, honey, citrus, woody, earthy, etc. was helpful and I am trying hard to express it exactly like that from time to time. (For detailed list of scent expressions refer to 'Reference: My own way of organizing fragrance expressions' below)

Now let's take a closer look at how to add scent to K-Sool.

Hwahyangipju Method and Jujungjiyak Method

|

Hints on how to add scent to K-Sool can be found in Director Park Rok dam's article on how to brew Songhwaju. There are two points: 'Hang songhwa in a mesh bag for 3 days before Chaeju' and 'Cut songhwa finely put it in a silk bag dig into the center 3 days before Chaeju and insert it'.

Here hanging method is called Hwahyangipju Method and inserting method is called Jujungjiyak Method. Those who are quick to notice the key to this method is '3 days before Chaeju'. If you put it too early or leave it for too long the scent becomes too strong and becomes worse than nothing.

Hwahyangipju Method @Naver Knowledge Encyclopedia Capture

There is a witty comment from Director Park in the same article:

With the thought of achieving what you want by borrowing someone else's strength "it's like a selfish brat" and "making alcohol is really easy"

I think' it's fun.

Various Sub-Ingredient Combinations

|

From the words of CEO Choi Young-eun who surprised many people by setting up a brewery in Gangnam with a unique name CMakgeolli we can see how to add taste and scent using various sub-ingredients. CEO Choi said that he had experimented with about 100 sub-ingredients when brewing alcohol at home which seems to be in line with Thierry Wasser's statement that basic scents are 3,000 and all must be known. Perhaps because he knows the characteristics of sub-ingredients well this is possible.

Various Makgeollis presented by CMakgeolli @CMakgeolli homepage capture

"There was a recent request for alcohol from an individual who requested wood scent, earth scent, fruit scent and acidity used as an aperitif. So I took out the alcohol that was in my head and made it using pear, bellflower and black tea. Because I had memories of the taste I made before I could easily combine them."

If you look at <Language of Scent> by Choi Nak-eon there are many reasons why scent is still difficult but the biggest factor is that the characteristics of scent(sub-ingredient) do not remain the same when mixed. In other words if you mix lavender and lemongrass half and half it doesn't mean that a harmonious middle scent with soft floral scent and refreshing lemon scent comes out.(In this respect CMakgeolli looks even more amazing.)

What sub-ingredients are commonly used to add scents to K-Sool in the Gayangju world other than commercial brewing? Hints can be obtained by analyzing the winning works of the 2020 Gayangju Brewer Selection Competition. In 2020 the competition was divided into Gahyang Yakju and Sungok Yakju and the winning works of Gahyang Yakju used hops, magnolia flower, tangerine peel, pine needles, songsun, lotus leaf, hwangchil tree, sweet flower, rose, Schisandra chinensis, Gapyeong pine nut, tangerine, apple etc. which far exceeded my expected spectrum so I thought it was really amazing. (For reference I put hops in and failed to advance to the finals.)

Smoking

|

Whiskey produced in Scotland is called Scotch whiskey and the biggest feature of Scotch whiskey is its smoky scent. The smoky scent comes from peat used to dry malt during peat but peat was actually an alternative fuel accidentally discovered by distillers who were worried about not having coal.

If you dry malt with peat smoke you get a smoky flavor as well as a strong flavor which leads to the identity of malt whiskey. There is no direct fire in K-Sool so it won't work with smoke but when steaming

Godubap or distilling when water or alcohol boils steam can add scent and putting sub-ingredients such as medicinal herbs in Godubap is already widely used.

Dry hopping

If you follow the history of beer, there isn't much to talk about without hops. Hops started as a natural preservative, but its unique bitterness balances the sweetness of malt, making it drinkable even when consumed in large quantities, and it is the key to opening up such a diverse world of beer.

I became interested in hops because of dry hopping, a method of

soaking hops in beer like tea bags after fermentation. I found something similar in 'Mannam-ui Gwangjang' Makgeolli from Gurumayang Brewery, which makes K-Sool with a unique personality.

"Since I was a latecomer, I had to try something different. I thought it would be difficult to differentiate with rice alone, so I thought about putting in sub-ingredients that others didn't put in. In the case of Samyangju Mannam-ui Gwangjang, pepper and ginger were added during the third fermentation. It's similar to dry hopping in craft beer." Ginger aside, pepper in it! I was amazed at the ideas of young brewers including Team Leader Yang Yumi.

Another place that uses a similar method is DOK Brewery. DOK Brewery has no end to its sub-ingredients such as pomegranate juice, black tea, lemon, lime, malt, and coffee in Makgeolli. Perhaps this part is backed by the experience of Representative Lee Min-gyu working at a world-famous craft beer company. So dry hopping probably wasn't unfamiliar.

Let's hear directly from Representative Lee.

"In the case of Korea traditional liquor, sub ingredients are put in together with Deos, sul during fermentation so the scent and taste of sub ingredients often volatilize during fermentation. Like dry hopping if you put flowers or fruit juice into alcohol after fermentation and cold soak it the characteristics remain more strongly in alcohol."

There is still much to learn about scents but hands must be ahead of head. Through various experiments I decided to narrow down my choices by gaining lessons.

★Experment 1:

What if I put edible essential oi in alcohol?

They say adding scent, what if I put scent directly into alcohol?

Personally, I like woody scents, which can be obtained through chemical synthesis, but cedarwood, sandalwood, and guaiacwood are obtained by directly heating and distilling wood. Unfortunately, there is no edible version, but instead I bought doTERRA's lemongrass essential oil, which is said to have a refreshing lemon scent.(Need to double check if it's edible!)

With high expectations, I put only a little bit into my alcohol and mixed it well and drank a glass… I almost vomited from the strong lemon scent that came up from deep inside(?) my body.(The scent lasted all day and came up every time I breathed.)

It would have been better to use a really small amount of essential oil and it was an oil type so it should have melted better in alcohol but it was an expensive experience to realize that drinking scent is completely different from smelling scent. That day my blog wrote how I felt at the time.

'A fresh but very dangerous attempt!'

Unfortunately, it doesn't seem like I'll try again.

★Experiment 2:

What if I smoke like Scotch whiskey?

Among the various attempts to add scent, smoking caught my eye. Is there a similar method for K-Sool? According to Director Ryu In-soo, if you put sub-ingredients in the rice or water under the pot when steaming Godubap, the scent will be absorbed.

If you think about it more, using roasted rice would also have the same effect. Oh good idea… Just as I was thinking about it, Yidaeap Brewery's 'Snowy Summer Night' Takju was released.

It is made by mixing non-glutinous rice and roasted glutinous rice and brewing three times. It is said that the richness of nurungji, the bitterness of coffee, the richness of nuts, and the acidity produced during fermentation are felt complexly. I was amazed at their experimental spirit and passion and crucially good timing.(Is it a coincidence? BREEZE & STREAM (Pungryu), a small-scale distillery startup established in April 2021, has its first product as Korea's first 'roasted' barley Soju.) I actually experimented with putting tea bags in water while steaming Godubap to add scent. Some of the scent flew away during fermentation but some of it remained until the end so I was surprised. It deserves serious application but it's still a shame that the scent flew away during fermentation.

★Experiment 3:

What if I blend with infused alcohol?

As mentioned briefly above, scents should be added after filtration or before bottling. If added early on, all scents will fly away due to carbon dioxide production. The most powerful way to capture scents is to dissolve them in alcohol. When solid sub-ingredients are placed in high-proof distilled alcohol, color, taste, and scent are absorbed through osmotic pressure. If you don't want color you can distill again to get better transparent infused alcohol with reduced impurities and off-flavors. This infused alcohol can be mixed with fermented alcohol to adjust the desired taste and scent like Spanish sherry wine which is famous for fortified wine.

I experimented with various ingredients. Hops(American), pine needles, lotus leaves, licorice root, herbs ginger stonecrop oak chips Osulloc tea bags 4 types. The method is simple. Divide pre-made distilled alcohol(Soju) put different ingredients in each for infusion then mix with fermented alcohol at about 20 degrees for a sensory evaluation combined tasting party.(For how to mix two alcohols to make them at desired degrees refer to <Korea traditional liquor textbook> Alcohol formula collection)

Various infusion experiments from 1 to 10

The results of combining various opinions are as follows.

First, herbs are the most effective ingredient for adding scents. There are already many herbs around us and they are familiar so alcohol blended with herb-infused alcohol received the best evaluation. There were many comments that it was high-class but it seems that people's perception of herb scents was reflected.

Second, tea bags are the most convenient ingredient for adding scents. I used several types of Osulloc tea bags which were already blended in various forms and just had to be put in so they were the easiest to use. However even though various ingredients were blended due to the characteristics of scents not everything appeared as expected which was unfortunate.

Third hops are quite good ingredients for adding scents but using them in pellet form is illegal. It's still strange why it's illegal but since natural hops are hard to come by unfortunately it seems difficult to use them in the future.

Fourth, for K-Sool commonly used pine needles, lotus leaves, mother chrysanthemum, ginger and sweet flag if the amount is a little too much the scent is too strong or bitter. Less is better than more. The appropriate amount of infusion ingredients left homework.

Fifth, oak scent reminded me of whiskey and had less resistance. Familiar scents seem to be connected to good images. For reference I used oak chips but there are two types French and American. French oak chips have a smooth and gentle oak scent and vanilla scent while American has more tannins and enhances spices or sweetness so keep that in mind.

Sixth, not a scent but from a comprehensive flavor perspective bitterness is commonly pointed out. Some people like high alcohol content and some find it burdensome. Soju used for infusion must be sufficiently aged and although the alcohol content will decrease the amount of mixing should be reduced. Or increasing sweetness or sourness to cover bitterness may also be one way.

★Experiment 4:
What if I use dry hopping?

Blending infused alcohol to add desired color, taste, and scent is a very attractive method, as proven in sherry wine. However, it requires appropriate quality distilled alcohol and a purpose and reason to withstand the increasing alcohol content, so it is difficult to see commonly.

Therefore, another way to add scent to fermented alcohol is needed, and that is dry hopping, which I introduced earlier.

At first, like what was used in 'Mannam-ui Gwangjan', I also tried putting pepper in finished alcohol. After putting about 5 whole peppers and waiting, it wasn't bad that the scent of pepper came up slightly through my nose.

Rather, I felt a spicy tingling sensation in my mouth, which was a unique experience and I

thought it would be worth applying in the future. As mentioned in the infusion blending, herbs are the best in terms of scent, but tea bags were convenient. Then I saw an interesting Wadiz funding, which is a collaboration between Kooksoondang sweet potato distilled alcohol Ryeo and Jirisan Hadong Ssanggye tea. 'Contrary to expectations, the subtle scent of tea rather highlighted the taste and scent of Ryeo, and the sweetness and fragrance of tea were further emphasized by Ryeo's taste and scent, achieving a perfect balance,' said the introduction. Although I haven't tasted it yet, it was enough to draw in my head with my past experience.

I don't know much about Ssanggye tea, but Osulloc that I drink occasionally was familiar. First of all, I looked at the characteristics of what was at hand. The first thing I saw was 'Ole full of cherry blossom scent, lemon verbena'. This tea with the subtitle 'Blended tea with bright cherry blossom scent from Jeju Island and sweet and sour fruit scent' contains Jeju black tea, rosehip fruit, pineapple sugar, hibiscus etc., and crucially contains 6.5% yellow cherry blossom scent mixture.

I don't know if you've ever tried it, but it was amazing that the flower scent and cherry scent were really strong but there was no taste at all. It's a tea just for scent.(According to reviews, there is a slight acidity and sweetness, but I may not have felt it because I put too much water. Hopefully no mistake) While at it, I also opened 'Sweet Bouquet Tea', which is introduced as 'a bright and sweet floral tea like a bride's bouquet'. Green tea 94.9% contains 5% sweet bouquet scent mixture, and when you take a close-up photo you can see pellets between green teas.

As it was made for the purpose of scenting, I thought it was perfect

Sweet Bouquet Tea (left), introduction text (middle), close-up photo(right)

for scenting. The problem is how to brew it and when to blend it. After looking into it a little more, cold brewing (brewing with cold water) seemed like a good idea. However, if left too long it becomes bitter and the unique stuffiness of green tea follows so within a day remove the tea bag and mix only a little bit of water before bottling. There are several tasting-related posts on my blog related to tea bag dry hopping so far. Here are just a few:

"It definitely has a peppermint scent. It's a little strong, scent feels out of balance

It's attractive!"

"Very light sweet scent. Sweet and savory taste and aroma. Weak bitterness at the end. Sweetness seems to reduce the bitterness."

"After drinking it a few days later, the scent of the tea bag seems to have gotten a little stronger. It would be better to reduce it a bit."

As mentioned when talking about scents when mixing scents the result prediction was not easy. In other words when mixing existing alcohol scents with tea bag scents some scents disappear completely while others become more prominent. From experience citrus scents seem to survive a lot.

Finally if I make K-Sool in this way will I get permission? Since I don't know much about this field I asked Kooksoondang's director Park Sunyoung for help thankfully she replied right away.

"If raw materials directly/indirectly affect alcohol(whether or not they seep into alcohol) they should be considered as raw materials for alcohol. The method you mentioned is also possible in this case you need to specify the product name of the tea bag and representative raw material name if the product name contains the product name of the tea bag you must specify its content in representative raw material name. I think it's possible."

So what about my K-Sool?

There are traditional methods such as hwahyangipju method or jujungjiyak method and various sub-ingredients are used to create taste and scent which is the recent trend but after various experiments dry hopping or infusion blending seems to be the best for me. In this regard I think I can produce any scent I want but strangely enough there is a strange counter-question in me whether alcohol with a scent that is prominent enough is good K-Sool.

Looking around us we are surrounded by artificially strong scents so this part naturally creates a gap between the scent that naturally comes from the original ingredients and the one that is artificially added. In the end this issue seems to be a problem of how to harmoniously (as if it is or not) melt various scents without harming the scent that naturally arises in the process of brewing K-Sool. It seems that more consideration and experimentation are needed.

•Reference•

My own way of organizing fragrance expressions

First of all, if a single fragrance comes out, approach it as one of **sweet, honey, floral, aromatic, fruity, or anise.**

1) Sweet scent when sugar is decomposed by heat or vanilla scent comes out sweet

2) Dense sweet scent like honey, if the scent of beekeeping honey comes out honey

3) Sweet scent of many flowers, if the scent of roses or jasmine comes out floral

4) Sweet scent of herbs such as coriander, basil and fennel, if the sweet scent of herbs comes out aromatic

5) Sweet scent of ripe fruit such as apples, bananas, grapes, melons, pears and pineapples fruity

6) Sweet scent with a smell like a Chinese medicine store, if the scent of octagonal or powdered stomach medicine in Chinese cuisine comes out anise

There are **balsamic** and **amber** that give a heavy feeling even though they are sweet scents.

1) Resin made by hardening tree sap, sweet and warm, balsamic with the smell that comes out in the cathedral
2) The scent of pumpkin, sweet resin that gives a warm feeling that stabilizes the mood if a heavy scent comes out amber

If the scent of wood, forest and nature comes out, it is one of **green, woody, mossy** or **earthy.**
1) A fresh and transparent scent reminiscent of green grass and leaves. If leaf scent comes out green
2) Woody or forest scent. If the smell of cut wood and warm wood scents such as cypress and cedar come out woody
3) Mossy scent on the surface of trees in deep forests. If moist and calm mossy scents on the floor come out mossy
4) The smell of dirt. If deep and calm scents come out earthy

Frequently used scents that are known by name alone. **Citrus, minty, herbal** and **spicy.**
1) The characteristic refreshing scent of citrus fruits. If lemon, orange, grapefruit, tangerine and lime scents come out citrus
2) Mint (peppermint) scent. If minty candy scents containing spearmint and mint come out minty
3) Herb-like scent. If lavender and rosemary representative scents come out herbal
4) Spicy scent like spices. If ginger, cumin and red pepper scents come out spicy

There are scents that are not often used but can be easily recognized. **marine** and **leather.**

1) A slightly fishy and metallic scent reminiscent of the sea or beach. If marine representative seaweed scent comes out

2) Leather smell. Animal-like smell reminiscent of tobacco smell. If leather product or new leather smell comes out leather

I grouped together scents that I don't know what they are just by looking at the words. **Musky, animalic, powdery, aldehyde.**

1) Musky: An adult-like fragrance with warmth and weight in an animallike atmosphere such as Chanel No. 5

2) Animalic: Although it has a deep odor concentration it has a warm feeling like flowers when diluted

3) Powdery: A light sweet fragrance reminiscent of white powder or dried powder with powdery flower fragrance

4) Aldehyde: A slightly sweet and fruity oily feeling from someone who is not drunk

In my experience there seems to be no field that requires as much study as fragrance. Usually our nose blocks familiar scents from the recognition process to reduce unnecessary fatigue. In other words there are many scents around you who are reading this article right now but you probably won't feel most of them. Therefore the ability to catch scents is very important. Let's expect new scents with an open mind and think about what kind of scents they might be when they pass by briefly. And to make that fragrance mine you have to give it a name. It could be one of the names written above or you could attach a familiar memory that you know well. That way the scent gradually becomes richer.

For those who are not familiar with K-Sool at the beginning of the book, I brewed Seogtanju together. Seogtanju, which uses ready-made Nuruk in a widely known recipe, was not bad with its sweet scent and sour taste, but somehow it seemed right to finish the book with Seolhwa-Oyangju using my own Nuruk.

If I talk about the process of brewing Seolhwa-Oyangju in detail, there will be no end to it, so I will try to solve it like I usually write on my blog.(Write it like a work diary.)

Title: Seolhwagog #23-4 Seolhwa-Oyangju Brewing
(#23-4 means the fourth Seolhwagog made in 23 years)

	Rice	Water	Nuruk	Four	Method	Remark
Jumo		2.0	1.3		1.5times water	Seolhwagog
Mitsul	0.5	1.0	Jumo	0.2	Beombeog	Add Jumo
Dose-sul1	1.0	2.0			Beombeog	
Dose-sul2	1.0	2.0	0.7		Beombeog	Add Seolhwagog
Dose-sul3	2.0				Glutinous Godubap	Add the divided Godubap
Dose-sul4	2.0	2.0			Non-Glutinous Godubap	After filtering
Total	6.5	7.0	2.0	0.2		
Ratio	1.0	1.1	30%	3%	← Relative to the amount of rice	

Recipe: Based on making Godubap 2kg at a time

Sunday, Jumo start

- Put 1.5 times water (2L) in 1.3kg of Seolhwagog

- Stir vigorously morning and evening

3rd day, boiling well

5th day, boiling less and yellow water on top

6th day, Mitsul
- Make Beombeog by pouring 1L of boiling water into 500g of nonglutinous
  rice flour
- When completely cooled, put it in Jumo and mix well
- Add 200g of wheat flour

Mitsul Day 1, opened before going to work and biling very well
- First Does-sul scheduled for 3 days later on 3/21

Deos-sul1 progress
- Make Beombeog by pouring 2L of boiling water into 1kg of nonglutinous
  rice flour
- When completely cooled, put it in Mitsul and mix well
- 2nd Deos-sul scheduled for 3 days later on 3/24

Deos-sul2 progress
- Make Beombeog by pouring 2L of boiling water into 1kg of nonglutinous
  rice flour
- When completely cooled, put it in Mitsul and mix well
- At this time, add an additional 700g of Seolhwagog (for saccharification)
- And then wash Glutinous rice 2kg and soak it in water (Sanjang start)
- 3rd Deos-sul scheduled for 3 days later on 3/27

Deos-sul3 progress
- Make Godubap with Glutinous rice that has been Sanjang for 3 days
- After the steam rises from the steamer, add glutinous rice drained and
  steam for 50 minutes
- Cool completely with a fan and put in a food canister
- Pour Mitsul into the food canister with Glutinous riceGodubap and mix

well with Godubap

- 4th Deos-sul scheduled for 7 days later on 4/3

Made Glutinous rice Godubap one day in advance for use in Deossul4

- Wash Non-glutinous rice 2kg well and make Godubap after draining water
- After steam rises from the steamer, steam for 1 hour, then sprinkle cold
  water and steam for another 20 minutes
- While Non-glutinous riceGodubap is being cooked, boil water(2L)
- Put Godubap in a food canister and pour boiling water
  immediately(Tanghon)
- Leave it as it is until it cools completely for more than a day

Deos-sul4 progress

- Open the food canister and squeeze out Deos-sul3
- Check if Non-glutinous rice Godubap made yesterday has cooled
  completely
- If confirmed to have cooled down, pour squeezed alcohol and mix well
-After 3 weeks, open on 4/24, look at the status, and decide on Chaeju

Chaeju when opened after 3 weeks because many grains have settled
down4/24

- Start low temperature aging and filtration of squeezed alcohol in
  refrigerator

Tasting after Chaeju a week

- Dilute further or separate clear alcohol
- If you want to add additional scent, use cold infusion with your favorite
  herbs Other than having many stages and a long period for Oyangju, the
  manufacturing method is simple because there are only Beombeog and

Godubap. On the other hand, there is a lot of room to apply different materials or methods at each stage, so there is a lot of flexibility, so I think it might be better to raise the level and brew alcohol.

The theme of the third Gungjungsul brewing contest in 2022 is Nuruk- Sool.

In addition, the Nuruk used must be submitted. I thought the timing wasexquisite. Because 2022 was a year when I focused on finding Seolhwagog that suits me all year round, and it was a time when I brewed more than 20 different Seolhwagog. I still couldn't find my own Nuruk that I liked, but I had plenty of Nuruk that I made. At this time, Nuruk-Sool felt like a topic that was released knowing my situation.

Nuruk-Sool contest winning Nuruks(mine is in the middle of the top row)

Many Seolhwagog used in experiments were difficult to use for various reasons, so eventually the 31st Seolhwagog made at the very end was used. It was made using the already familiar Oyangju method and did not adjust the taste or add fragrance specially according to last year's lesson.

Fortunately, I was selected as a finalist and on the subway heading to Bangbae-dong, I suddenly thought that it would be fortunate if I could receive a commendation award. Because I know my skills. When I arrived at the institute, 18 Yakju and Nuruk that advanced to the main round were on display.

I carefully tasted one by one and carefully examined Nuruk. There were some that used ready-made Nuruk, but many K-Sools used hand-made Nuruk, and especially, there were 6 rice Nuruk, which was impressive. The taste and scent of works were evenly good, but there were only about 3 that could be pointed out as better, so I suddenly thought that I might have a chance to win.

What was interesting was that a woman who happened to be tasting mine asked the man who came with her, "Honey, doesn't this alcohol smell like something?" (Of course she didn't know that I made that.) After tasting it once or twice more, I heard her say, "It smells like pineapple!" I didn't show it off, but I was 'very very' happy inside.

When my name wasn't called until the silver prize, I thought it wouldn't work this time. But when my name was called at the gold prize, all my efforts passed like a horse lantern. I thought this day would come for me, no, it finally came and I was grateful for all these things. It's like someone handing me a glass of cold water when I'm about to fall from exhaustion.

(Out of nowher) One scene from the manga Ben Hur @Klhyang capture

Later, I requested and received the judging results. Unlike last year, there were no detailed judging results by category, but the judges' evaluations were specific and well expressed.

Judges' Evaluation

Judge 1 : Slight turbidity / Grain scent and melon scent with sweetness / Light sweetness and weak sourness with vanilla scent in the aftertaste and light throat feel make it a balanced alcohol.

Judge 2 : The degree of Nuruk fermentation or the state of the law is very good. The color, taste and scent of alcohol are all excellent overall. The aftertaste is a bit weak, but it would be nice to improve it.

Judge 3 : There is a maturation scent and a slightly greasy taste, a heavy body feel and sourness while being bitter, but the slightly greasy taste is attractive

Judge 4 : Clean sweetness is attractive and the scent is excellent / The bitter aftertaste of alcohol should be delayed or aged longe

Part of the judging results of the 2022 Gungjungsul brewing contest

He melon scent is a typical Seolhwagog scent and my alcohol usually has almost no acidity, but thanks to using Sanjang for the first Godubap, it seems to have received good reviews in terms of balance. There is a point that the end taste is bitter, but I think it can be improved through aging.

Finishing the competition entry

|

The K-Sool competition, which started with the level of alcohol I made, has reached 12 times in terms of number of times and 5 years in terms of years. A light challenge sometimes becomes a goal and there are difficult times, but looking back, I think I did really well. In the future, as long as 'I receive a grand prize and my qualifications are not suspended', I plan to continue. The reasons are as follows.

When I brew K-Sool and share it with acquaintances, I often ask how it is, but free of charge alcohol always tastes good so it's hard to get an objective evaluation. In this situation, having an objective and formal evaluation opportunity is meaningful even if you pay an entry fee. (Depending on the competition, they even give rice so they should be grateful enough to bow.) If you make an entry as much as you can or if you can't do it as much as you can't do it, why did such a result come out? In the process of worrying about this, you can identify the weaknesses of my alcohol and crucially know the public's taste. Various entry experiences lead to questions about what good alcohol is and help design various recipes. It doesn't take one or two days to brew in one go, so you have to plan your alcohol at least on a quarterly basis and maintain tension throughout. This part is the driving force behind improving your brewing skills. Plus if you even win a prize you get a small prize money which makes you happy and above all it's a huge help in managing your K-Sool brewing career. Even if you look closely at Janghido-ga, Geumgyedang, Yangjugol-gaKorea traditional liquor, J&J Brewery, Byeongyeongyangjo, Gachi Brewery House, Soolawon Brewery House , Soolsaem Brewery House , Naeoldam Brewery House etc., it's not an exaggeration to say that all these powerful brewery representatives have made connections through K-Sool competitions.

Therefore I will continue to challenge K-Sool competitions in the future. And for many amateur brewers who are thinking of challenging them I hope my experience will be helpful.

What will happen in the future?

More diverse and more experiments

|

In my own Nuruk episode, I showed various Seolhwagog manufacturingrelated experiments, but there are still many things to try. A representative example is to see the changes in the Seolhwa-Oyangju manufacturing process and the difference in flavor due to changes in materials. Initially, I tried using glutinous rice and black rice as Seolhwagog ingredients, but I couldn't properly organize them due to various experiments. Even if the main ingredient is fixed as non-glutinous rice, I am curious about what difference it will make to the actual alcohol when brewed by distinguishing various sub-ingredients.

I am also very interested in the environment for making Seolhwagog. I am currently using a stanless shiru, but although there is paper on the side, it is vulnerable to moisture because it is in contact with rice flour.

I wonder if better results will come out if boxes are added to facilitate moisture discharge. And I also want to improve the drying facility. If you stack a large amount at once and dry it, it will stick together and postfermentation will occur, so it is best to spread it as thinly as possible. To do this, many large trays are needed and a structure that stacks upwards is required. I would like to have a dedicated device optimized for drying so that the dried Seolhwagog powder does not fly as much as possible.

Various experiments are also needed for Seolhwa-Oyangju. Currently, there is only a basic recipe, but first of all, I want to experiment with whether various K-Sools with different characteristics can be brewed by changing the ingredients of the last Deos-sul with the DaJumo method, adjusting the processing method, whether or not there are subingredients, and whether or not there is fragrance.

Winning the highest award at K-Sool Contest
|

As promised in the text, I intend to continue participating in the K-Sool Contest. Participating in a contest gives tension to brewing alcohol and brings vitality to life by arousing an active mind and challenging spirit. So if possible, I want to receive the highest award at all contests. By then, turn your eyes overseas…

My brewery startup worries
|

The subtitle of this book 'Finding My Own Nuruk' is 'No Your Own Nuruk, No Your Own Brewery'. It means that I can make a brewery because I have my own Nuruk, so I am planning a next book called 'My

Brewery Startup Story'. There are still many shortcomings to start a brewery, but I have many thoughts about what it would look like if I started a brewery.

Originally, I was going to put everything in one book, but I accepted the advice from the surroundings that Nuruk's story and brewery startup worries do not match each other and decided to divide it into two.

Starting with general procedures and necessary things related to brewery startup, who I want to sell my K-Sool to, how to brew my K-Sool if I brew it in a brewery instead of an apartment, how much would be appropriate if I put a price on my K-Sool, and if it's not for drinking and getting drunk but for making K-Sool that people want to buy even if it costs money, what kind of appearance should it be? I'm thinking of putting these stories in. If you read this book interestingly and usefully, please look forward to the next book.

It's time to end the long text. I'm going to finish the book with a passage from a book called <Second Business Card> that I saw before.

"In the past, I thought I had to find something I could do with passion. But now that I think about it, passion wasn't discovered but was created while working. Most people don't put in effort until they master something and passion springs up. The myth of passion is the biggest reason why my friends are not satisfied with their jobs."

Finding My Own Nuruk

No Your Own Nuruk, No Your Own Brewery

Written by Kim Hyuck-Rae

How is K-Sool made?
What is good K-Sool?
What kind of K-Sool do I want to make?

BOOKK

Contents

'Finding My Own Nuruk', written like martial arts novel. Who can write a book like this?

Most books talk about success, but this book talks about failure. As if revealing the living room of the house, we put together all the experiences of what efforts were made to overcome failures and who they left in search of. This is 'Finding My Own Nuruk' by Kim HyuckRae.

In the book, K-Sool is likened to Go. 'K-Sool 18th grade' is a very interesting metaphor. Perhaps those new to K-Sool want to make K-Sool as delicious as a Go master. However, masters do not become masters by making K-Sool for a long time, but those who make fewer mistakes become masters.

At events such as the K-Sool graduation ceremony and Korea Gayangju Research Institute, Director Ryu In-soo's praise for thank you and thank you is always overflowing, but I never thought I would say such a hot-faced word. Um… Aside from that, Director Ryu In-soo. This book could not have come into the world without your help. I bow my head and thank you for borrowing this space and ask for your continued guidance.(… It's still very awkward. J) In addition, I would like to express my gratitude to Park Sun-young, head of Kooksoondang, Han Young-seok, director of Han Young-seok's Fermentation Research Institute, and Kim Jae-hyung, director of Korea Liquor Literature Research Institute. These people always